BON VOYAGE!

A Susie Kelly Sampler

BON VOYAGE!

A Susie Kelly Sampler

Blackbird Digital Books
London
2013

Blackbird Digital Books
London 2014
First published by Blackbird Digital Books 2014
© Susie Kelly 2014
The moral right of the author has been asserted.
Cover artwork: *Romantic girl in a red dress* c. Medusa, Dreamstime.com
Cover design by Elite Cover Artwork Factory
ISBN-13: 978-1495221736 ISBN-10: 1495221733

CONTENTS

INTRODUCTION

In the early months of 2010 I was just setting up my little online publishing company, Blackbird Digital Books, and blogging about my progress when I received an email submission, my first ever, from Susie. She wondered if I might be interested in publishing her new book. Her UK sales were good (and how, 50,000+ with Transworld), she explained, but she'd never been published in the USA and felt there might be an audience for her work there. The sample she sent was about a 500-mile cycling trip she and her husband had taken through the little-known Marne and Champagne regions of Northern France. I was hooked from the first page. It wasn't only a very funny travel tale but also a fascinating history lesson as they followed in the footsteps of Marie-Antoinette and King Louis XVI on their unsuccessful attempt to flee the guillotine.

As a writer I've had my share of rejection letters. The line that used to crop up again and again was "great story, great writing etc but *I just didn't love it enough* to take it on." I now understand this sentiment so well. I was lucky enough to find deep and lasting love right from the getgo. I am a huge fan of Susie's work, I think she's one of the funniest, most engaging, most empathetic writers I've ever come across. I love her and I love her books and they keep on coming and they keep on surpassing themselves. Her latest, *I Wish I Could Say I Was Sorry...* (May 2013) is simply a masterpiece of memoir-writing. Early reviewers, fans who have already discovered Susie's books about France, are wholeheartedly agreeing. I've cried at movies before but never at a book. The proofreader too, a "roughty toughty bloke" as he describes himself, and a fellow-fan, declared that he hadn't cried at a book since Dickens. It's a departure from her normal light-hearted comedy, but her sense of fun is still there, always there, as the shocking revelations continue to build.

Blackbird Digital Books has been growing slowly but we are still a tiny publisher and don't have advertising budgets as such - yet - hence this anthology. It's brought to you as a showcase; to spread the word about Susie's wonderful lighthearted companionship in her words. The opening chapters of her astonishing memoir are included.

Susie is on all the social media sites - Twitter, Facebook etc and loves engaging with her readers. If you enjoy what you find here, please don't be shy about getting in touch with her. The links are at the back of this book. Like me, you might just find yourself with a rather special new friend.

Bon voyage!

Stephanie Zia
Editor, Blackbird Digital Books

1
TRAVELS WITH TINKERBELLE
6,000 Miles Around France In A Mechanical Wreck

The author and her husband devised a simple plan – to take a tent and the dog and drive around the perimeter of France. Like many simple plans it went wrong before it started and they ended up with two dogs and a campervan named Tinkerbelle. On the second day of their journey Tinkerbelle begins to self-destruct, helped by the new dog who does his best to eat her from the inside out. This is their story, as they travel from sandy beaches to snow-topped mountains exploring the diverse cultures, cuisines and countryside making up the country called France.

There's a reason the inhabitants of the Poitou-Charentes are affectionately known as *cagouilles* – snails. It's rare to see anybody moving faster than a cautious walking pace. Only mad foreigners jog. A common denominator in the obituaries is the great age of the departed – mid to late 90s is pretty much the norm. Some of our French neighbours have never been more than 30 miles from the village where they were born. Their needs and wants can generally be found in small local towns; why should they go further afield?

The same indolence affects us. With quaint villages, traffic-free lanes, limitless acres of fields, forests and rivers, long hot summers, sufficient hostelries to cater for our tastes, and the pure pleasure of sitting in the garden surrounded by our animals, listening to the birds, we live in our own little heaven.

But in this paradise there is a sly serpent, and its name is Wanderlust. When it whispers I feel a craving to be on the move.

"Shall we take Tally," (our dog) "and a tent, and drive all round France? Just drive around and see what we can discover?" I suggested one autumn day while we were collecting chestnuts.

"When?" Terry asked.

"Late spring, early summer?"

"How long for?"

"About six weeks?"

"All right. Find somebody to come and look after the animals, and we'll go."

What could be simpler? All we needed was a house-pet-sitter and a tent.

I contacted our lovely American friend, Jennifer Shields who had taken care of our animals and house some years previously when I had walked across France. She'd be delighted to come back, so that was one thing ticked off our list.

"Do you think," I asked, "that Tally will get bored being in the car for so long? Should we get a small companion for him?"

Yes, we agreed, that would be a good idea. And so we collected a small black puppy of unknown origin who looked like the kind of small black puppy who would grow to be a small black dog. His huge ears, instant devotion and tireless efforts to please reminded me of Dobby the house-elf in Harry Potter, and so that's what we called him.

Two months before our departure date, things began to go awry.

Firstly Jennifer badly injured her leg and had to cancel her visit.

Secondly, Dobby grew, and grew, and grew. In no time at all he was the size of a new-born calf. He wasn't going to fit in our car with Tally, all our camping gear, and us. We were going to have to buy a far larger vehicle. One that we couldn't afford.

In a serendipitous stroke of fate, my old schoolfriend from Kenya, Vivien Prince, won a raffle prize – an open-ended return flight from Kenya to Paris. She enthusiastically volunteered to step into Jennifer's shoes.

Buying a vehicle large enough to accommodate our equipment and canine entourage, and that was within our means, was more difficult. With Vivien already here, and only six days before our departure date, we still hadn't found anything we could afford. At the eleventh hour, somebody introduced us to an ageing Talbot van converted to a campervan. She was beautifully fitted with hand-made oak cabinets and seemed mechanically sound. She cost more than twice what we had budgeted for, but she was our only option. We were ready to roll.

NORTHERN BRITTANY
Ille et Vilaine

We are starting our trip from Cancale on the Brittany coast, and will travel 6,000 miles anti-clockwise around the perimeter of France until we arrive back where we began.

On a chilly day in May we wave farewell to Vivien and head north from our home in south-west France. It is 250 miles to Cancale, and we reach a campsite near there late at night after a pleasant and uneventful journey, apart from Terry finding that the clutch is rather stiff. We quietly park Tinkerbelle, drink cups of instant soup, wrap the dogs and ourselves in duvets, and fall asleep.

The first morning of our trip is off to a sublime start. At 8.00am the sun is already hot. From a gentle incline on the Pointe du Grouin north of Cancale, we overlook the sapphire waters of the bay of Mont-Saint-Michel to the east and the gulf of St Malo to the west. Just offshore a babbling mass of gulls and cormorants flap and hop about on the Île des Landes.

I join a queue of cheerful French folk in dressing gowns and slippers as we wait to wash our dishes in the communal facilities. There is a single topic of conversation – the glorious weather. A small, nut-brown man wearing a striped blue-and-white jumper and tiny white shorts pronounces with an air of authority that we are witnessing the beginning of a long hot summer. We all gaze at him with the reverence that the faithful in St Peter's Square might regard the Pope.

Although the inside of Tinkerbelle, as we have named the campervan, is a muddled mess, we will sort it out later. First things first: this is a holiday. We take the dogs to walk along the cliff top. They are astonished by their first sight of the sea, undecided whether to rush back and forth on the path or scale the cliffs down to the water that lies below, as flat and still as a blue sheet of glass. This is the Brittany coastline at its most docile and beguiling, bearing no resemblance to the familiar postcard scenes of titanic waves engulfing lighthouses and ships.

With the dogs sprawling comfortably on our bed in the back of the van, we point Tinkerbelle towards St Malo. On the way we stop at a perfect sandy beach where the only other occupants are a couple with a small child and a golden retriever. Tally rushes over to play, but Dobby is entranced by his first introduction to the sea. He lies down in it and gulps mouthfuls of salt water for several minutes before joining the two dogs racing around the rocks and kicking up the sand. Half an hour later the quantity of sea-water he's drunk have a predictably unsettling effect upon his digestion.

After he's recovered we continue on our way, until we notice a sign to 'Les Rochers Sculptés' at Rothéneuf. We pick our way down a twisty, stony path to a colony of monsters, smugglers and corsairs sprawling in the sun on a windy hillside overlooking the ragged Emerald Coast. These strange creatures are the work of a 19th century local priest. For 25 years this lonely man passed his spare time here sculpting from the granite several hundred intricate figures, based upon the legend of a powerful 16th century Rothéneuf family of pirates and smugglers. There are sea-calves, serpents, stern watchmen, and figures eroded past recognition. My favourite is a rectangular tableau showing what looks like a couple of dwarves against a background of palm trees. The male dwarf appears to be simultaneously pulling off the lady's headdress and kicking her up the backside.

Old photographic postcards show the Abbé's handiwork in its heyday, before time and tide and the tramp of feet had taken their toll. I wonder what he'd been thinking as he chipped away for all those years, and how long his lonely labour of love will last before the elements obliterate it.

The cobbled streets and battlements of St Malo are crammed with vehicles and holidaymakers. Flags swoon limply in the still heat. We will not stay here overnight; it's too busy. We are looking for somewhere remote and quiet, where the dogs can run free. Tinkerbelle's gears are making a horrible grinding noise, and there is a loud rattling coming from somewhere beneath the bodywork.

Côtes d'Armor

Until 1959 the *département* in which we are now was called the Côtes-du-Nord – the northern coast. Bretons felt it was misleading and damaging to tourism, which after agriculture is their main source of revenue. 'Nord' suggested cold, but the Bretons regard their climate as mild; and whilst it is indisputable that Brittany is in the northern region of France, it does lie to the west. And so the Côtes-du-Nord became the more seductive Côtes-d'Armor. Pale blue sky, pink stones, bleached white sands. Yachts clinking and jingling on their moorings. Collections of quaint stone cottages nestling in clumps of rhododendrons and semi-tropical vegetation. The tide is far out, and gulls poke about for morsels in an inlet of glossy mud.

Every turn in the road reveals another glorious beach of pristine sand tickled by a silky turquoise sea. Beside the lighthouse at Cap Fréhel we are nearly blown off our feet and the edge of the cliff by the ferocity of a wind that arrives from nowhere, and which is not only ferocious but also freezing, but Tally and

Dobby are oblivious as they gallop around through the beautiful moorland heather and wild flowers.

We pass the small town of Minihy-Tréguier where St Yves, patron saint of lawyers, was born into a noble family. After training as a priest he studied law and devoted himself to helping the underprivileged. Defending a poor man sued for having the impudence to stand outside a kitchen enjoying the cooking smells, for which the smells' owner felt he was entitled to payment, Yves rattled a coin. The noise, he said, paid for the smell. I like that!

It is almost 7.00pm when we reach Ploumanac'h, where there are, according to an apparently reliable directory, three open campsites. The first two are closed. Terry is tired and irritable after wrestling all day with Tinkerbelle's gearbox which is becoming exceedingly temperamental and will no longer engage reverse, and we are both hungry. We've driven several times up and down and round and round in Ploumanac'h and are barely speaking by the time we eventually stumble upon the third campsite. Terry finds the traffic too slow, the signs useless and the other drivers idiots, and apparently it's entirely my fault. While we set up the awning, feed and walk the dogs I maintain a righteous frosty silence until Terry invites me to a meal at Trégastel-Plage.

Terry enjoys oysters followed by *moules* and *frites*, while my prawns, salmon and chilled rosé perfectly match the pink blush of the boulders squatting on the beach in the final rays of the sun. The Pink Granite Coast is at its very pinkest, and its rosy beauty melts away our irritability. It's a perfect evening.

The following morning we discover that during the night Dobby has eaten Tally's collar. A cold wind (it is definitely cold despite the mild Breton climate) lashes an improbably green sea into curly white-tipped waves, on which a lone yacht rocks and bobs. We cross the *départementale* boundary into Finistère, literally 'the end of the earth'.

Finistère

According to an article in the Brittany Tourist Board's magazine, the town of Morlaix prides itself on being the home of possibly the oldest chili palm in Europe, even the world, standing 65 ft. tall and bearing 12 ft. long leaves. We imagine the palm rearing up over the town like a vast parasol, but there is no sign of it. We go to ask about it at the Tourist Office, which closes for lunch as we arrive at its door.

There's a small créperie in a sheltered sunny square facing a row of tall houses, where gulls dance among the self-sown plants on saggy slate roofs. After lunching on Breton *galettes* and golden Breton cider, we wander down a quaint cobbled alley and into l'Echoppe Artisanale, a hat shop of extraordinary beauty. Confections of straw and ribbons, chiffon and silk, flowers, artificial fruits and jewels, so light, so colourful, so luscious that they'd be at home in a Parisian *patisserie*. If you want a beautiful hat, try this shop first.

At 2.00pm we head back to the Tourist Office.

"We'd like to see your famous chili palm," I explain to the girl at the counter. "Could you tell us where to find it, please?"

"Ah yes, there are many chili palms. You can see them in Roscoff."

"We'd like to see the one in Morlaix – the one mentioned in your brochure." I show her the magazine article from the *Comité Départemental du Tourisme du Finistère* mentioning the great palm. She reads it, looking nonplussed.

"Well, I don't know where that palm is," she says, "so it's probably privately owned and not open to the public."

"Are you sure? Could you possibly find out whether we can go and see it?"

"No, I'm afraid not." She turns her attention to a pile of booklets on a shelf behind her.

"We've come quite a long way especially to see the tree. Perhaps you could suggest how we can find out how to view it?"

"Yes," she replies. "Go to Roscoff."

Back in Tinkerbelle, the traffic lights turn red as we approach. Terry brakes, and Tinkerbelle gives a despairing shudder and makes a very bad clunking sound.

"Oh, hell," I say. "Has somebody hit us, or have we burst a tyre?"

Terry climbs out and walks round to the back, where he stands looking perplexed. In the rear-view mirror I see the driver of the car behind us waving to him, and pointing. Terry lies down in the road and vanishes under Tinkerbelle, shortly reappearing with a length of exhaust pipe. The lights change to green and cars behind hoot, their drivers smiling and waving as they pass.

My heart sinks. On the second day of our trip, there is already a gearbox problem, a clutch problem and now a broken exhaust. We have bought a mechanical wreck! Is the entire vehicle going to fall to bits? The unexpected need to buy a camping car because of the small black puppy has already eaten up nearly all the funds we had put aside for our journey. There is no margin for major emergencies.

"Don't worry, it's no problem," Terry reassures me in his characteristically positive way. "We'll just keep going for now, and as soon as we find a breaker's yard we'll pick up a used part."

Off we drive, noisily. The lush vegetation, narrow winding lanes, pretty stone cottages and Celtic road signs are reminiscent of Cornwall. To our right the inshore waters of the beautiful bay of Morlaix are palest turquoise, darkening by shades into the distance to a deep aquamarine.

Local place names beginning with Plou-, Tré-, and Lan- reflect the fact that the Breton language is a sister to Welsh and Cornish. Between the 5th and 7th centuries Christians fleeing Anglo-Saxon persecution in England came to Armorique, the land of the sea. They called their new home Brittany, or Little Britain. That's why England, Scotland and Wales became known, in the 17th century, as Great Britain.

Terry mentions that Tinkerbelle's gearbox seems to have eased up. However, he adds casually, the brakes aren't quite as effective as they should be. He says I shouldn't worry, so I try not to. We drive past fields of artichokes and potatoes stretching right to the horizon, and to the horizon beyond that.

Roscoff is quaint and picturesque, touristy but charming, the harbour front lined with slate-roofed stone cottages. People drift around in the sunshine through narrow streets, and a bridge disappears into the sea. We drive around looking in vain for giant chili palms, before giving up and driving to Sainte-Marguerite on the Coast of Legends, where we find a stunningly beautiful location in the dunes of the Abers. Gulls float overhead, and a single red-sailed fishing boat skirts the rocks. We drop anchor for the night and take the dogs down to the beach, where patches of seaweed as red as the sail form a playground for legions of sand hoppers.

A black Labrador on a lead watches wistfully as Tally and Dobby race across the sand and rocks, while we collect smooth, tactile pebbles in subtle colours. But we don't take them away, because I always feel that stones removed from their natural environment lose their soul, and never look as perfect anywhere else.

As dusk falls and the dogs have run until they can't run any more we make our way back from the beach. A well-camouflaged green and buff-coloured toad tuts indignantly as it scrambles clumsily out of our way on the sandy path.

Our morning and evening ritual is labour-intensive. During the day, while we are travelling the dogs stay in the back of the van, sitting on what at night will become our bed. It's two benches facing each other, with a table between. The table collapses on request, and with some rearranging the cushions form a mattress that we cover with a thick blanket for the dogs. At night, they sleep in the cab. Once they are removed from the back, we can cook a meal, eat at the table, and then drag out from various drawers our bed linen and such other things as are necessary for our comfort. From whichever part of the van they are occupying we have to remove everything chewable: camera, maps, guide books, pens, mobile phones, ropes are all grist to Dobby's insatiable mill. It is an immutable fact that if it's within his reach he will eat it, despite the fact that we have brought with us sufficient dog toys to stock a small shop. In the three days since we left home he has devoured amongst other things a washing up bowl and sponge, a pair of socks and a plastic container screwed to the wall, as well as chewing Tally's collar into four sections. Each morning we stow away everything in the back, make up the bed with the dogs' blanket and their toys and put their water bowl down. They are happy to wrestle and snooze until the next opportunity for a run.

The night is still and silent, the darkness pierced by the white light of Europe's tallest lighthouse, the Phare de l'Île de la Vierge.

WEST & SOUTHERN BRITTANY
Finistère

Next morning is heralded not by the song of the larks, but by the persistent rapping of a woodpecker. The dogs leap from the cab, full of *joie de vivre* and hurtle straight into a neighbouring campervan that arrived during the night. A small angry poodle shocks them and sends them racing down to the beach. They spend the next hour chasing each other over the sands and through the dunes while we breakfast. They are like children in their delight at this new experience, running back to us every few minutes to make sure we are still here, and to tell us how much fun they are having. We rub off as much wet sand as we can before they jump back onto the bed and we set off for another day.

We've no plan other than to wander along the coast and see what we find. The villages have comic-book names - Ar Stonk, Kroaz Konk. Around every curve is a new paradise, the beaches of dreams, the beaches of childhood memories. No busy promenades, ice-cream vendors or deckchairs. Just pepper-fine silver sands patterned with birds' footprints and sprinkled with small, delicate shells, lapped by clearest waters beneath cloudless skies.

Bedding flutters from windows, taking advantage of the sunshine and nippy breeze. There's a hairdressing salon named Marine Hair, where the mermaids go when they need a new style. Platoons of cyclists in bright-coloured tight clothing whirr past as we chug for several miles down narrow lanes behind a tractor loaded with new potatoes and fragrant cattle-shed cleanout, a rural scent that I love, while appreciating that it's not for everyone.

We stop for coffee at a smart beach-side restaurant. The ladies' room is down some steep stairs in a narrow basement. A large lady on crutches is struggling to negotiate the steps, so another lady and I take her by the elbows and manoeuvre her to the bottom. While waiting for her to emerge, the other lady and I discuss the superb weather, wondering if it is too good to be true (it is), and whether it will last through the summer (it won't). All the time we are standing there the chef in his whites is hopping up and down the stairs collecting boxes of oysters from an open storage area next to the loo. Sometimes it's better not to see behind the scenes in restaurants.

Across the sea to our right lies the Île d'Ouessant, a haven for lighthouses and home to one with an interesting history, La Jument. In March of 1904 M. Charles Eugene Potron, who had survived a shipwreck, bequeathed a large sum of money for the erection of a lighthouse. It was to be of the highest quality and fitted with the finest equipment, and built on a rock in some of the most dangerous waters of the Atlantic coastline, off the Île d'Ouessant. M. Potron's Will stipulated that if the lighthouse wasn't completed within seven years, the legacy would become void and would pass instead to the Central Society for the Shipwrecked.

The site chosen for the new lighthouse was an area of one hundred square yards of rock, only accessible during calm weather and at low tide. Construction began in May 1904 in diabolical conditions, and during the first year only 51 hours of work were accomplished. The La Jument lighthouse was finally completed just before the seven year deadline. Twenty years later somebody noticed that it wasn't anchored to the rock, but simply perched on top and maintained in place by its own weight. Since then it has been secured by four high-tension cables.

It's market day in picturesque le Conquet, or if you prefer its funny Breton name, Konk Leon. The town is throbbing with holidaymakers and strutting dogs. Tinkerbelle splutters and farts through the crowded streets, startling shoppers at stalls selling strawberries, pillows, fish, cheeses and vegetables, fabrics and jewellery, and bread in every possible shape. Once she is tucked into a car park we take the dogs to explore the port where the morning's catch had been unloaded and despatched in the early morning. A few fishermen are picking out tiny crabs and small useless fish who have died needlessly in the awful nylon nets that have replaced traditional linen and cotton.

From Denis Lunven's *boulangerie* in Rue Clemenceau we buy two glossy slabs of *kuign aman* - literally 'butter cake', a Breton speciality made with lashings of butter, heaps of sugar and a teeny sprinkling of flour just sufficient to bind it together. We also buy a cake with a layer of seaweed in it. We like new tastes. Close by is a café/bar where we sit in the sun at a table on the pavement. Terry is drinking his coffee and I am sipping cider as we munch our way through the cakes. Seeing a small, self-important dog swaggering about bringing the traffic to frequent abrupt halts, heedless of its own safety and the irritation of drivers, Dobby makes a sudden lunge in a frenzied attempt to join in the fun, almost dragging us and our table into the middle of the road.

Saturated with buttery cakes we drive to St Mathieu's Point, where there's a ruined abbey, a lighthouse and a monument to sailors who have given their lives for France. Built by Benedictine monks, and facing Jerusalem in accordance with tradition, the abbey is dedicated to St Matthew, patron saint of tax collectors and accountants. Breton sailors brought a piece of his skull here from Ethiopia, where he either died naturally or was martyred in the course of squeezing taxes out of people. Nobody knows how he met his end. If you examine a set of apostle spoons you'll see that each of the apostles holds something in his hand. St Matthew holds an axe. Don't you think that's a strange tool for a tax collector?

Elegant arches stand in the broken walls of the abbey, and granite pillars reach up searching for a roof that is no longer there. Even in its skeletal state the abbey retains a suggestion of its lost grandeur. Now pigeons nest in the dark and dank mossy walls of the dormitory. There's nobody here on this wild headland except us, and the air carries the haunting sadness of a once mighty place reduced to lonely emptiness. In a walled field where once the monks grew vegetables and fruit, medicinal plants and fodder for their animals, a blackbird feeds her fluttering baby amongst the buttercups.

50,000 ships pass here each year, through one of the world's busiest maritime crossroads. From the extreme edge of the cliffs and tucked up tight against the abbey, Saint Mathieu's lighthouse peers down, incongruously, through the open roof space. Nearby is the stone chapel of Notre Dame du Bout du Monde – Our Lady of the End of the World - a simple building with a high vaulted ceiling, plain stone walls, and pots of agapanthus and arum lilies on the altar before a statue of the Madonna.

As we meander along we see a sign to a strawberry museum at Plougastel-Daoulas. I am intrigued to learn how a whole museum can be centred on a strawberry, but Terry drives past, apparently deaf to my suggestion. He's alternately pumping the clutch and brakes up and down.

The spectacular bay of Douarnenez is the site of the legendary city of Ys, built by the king of Cornouailles for his evil daughter Dahut. Every night Dahut took a new lover whom she forced to wear a silken mask. At daybreak the mask turned into a horrible clawed creature that killed its wearer, whose body was thrown into the sea. Fittingly, Dahut died as a result of her treachery when she opened the gates of Ys and flooded the city. It's said that in March, when the tides reach their nadir, the ruins of palaces can be seen in the sands, and on a quiet night you may hear the city's bells tolling.

Heading towards Plogoff we find a simple campsite - just a small field behind the house - belonging to a dear old lady who keeps a public bar in her tiny front room. As well as alcohol she sells packets of biscuits, jars of coffee, tins of vegetables, and very old postcards. We have a glass of cider with two locals who ask if we are going to visit the Pointe du Raz. We ask how far it is to walk, and the two customers and landlady all point in conflicting directions and give distances ranging from a quarter of a mile to six miles, and times ranging from ten minutes to four hours. We decide to postpone our visit until tomorrow, and to drive there, because we don't actually know exactly where we are, and if we leave on foot we might never find our way back. There is no road sign at either end of the hamlet, and when we ask its name they all talk at once and give different answers, and it sounds as if they are saying that the place doesn't actually have a name.

Apart from a young couple in a tent who look suspiciously like a pair of schoolchildren enjoying an illicit weekend together when their parents think they are studying at a friend's house, we have the campsite to ourselves. The only sounds are of a blackbird chattering in the hedge, and the methodical munching of cattle in a neighbouring field.

This morning our hostess asks us to walk down the lane to admire the quaint local chapel. It has just been rebuilt from a virtual ruin, she explains, paid for by fund-raising events organised by the local community who are immensely proud of it. It is a charming, simple little building with a smart new timber ceiling and decorated with naïve paintings. If only it had a name on it, we might be able to discover where we are. But it doesn't, so we are doomed never to know.

We drive about until we find a sign to the Pointe du Van, a site of unbelievable, unspoilt beauty carpeted in grasses and herbs, heathers and wild flowers. Granite boulders pierce clumps of pink scabious that perfectly complement the blues of the sea and sky. No words or photographs can capture the essence of its magical beauty. The sky and the sea are linked by a dozen shades of blue. Standing at the cliff's edge looking out at the Atlantic Ocean, on a perfect early summer day when the sea is calm and there's not another human being in sight, and the only sound is of lazy waves tickling the rocks, you'll believe you can fly.

Instead of their usual wild gallop the dogs move slowly, sniffing the air and staring around them in wonderment as we trace the path to the chapel of St They, which stands perilously close to the clifftops. This is mainland France's most westerly place of worship. Outside on a granite pillar two characters stand back to back, but the inscription has been worn away by time. Lizards scuttle round the stone window openings and over the lichen-covered slates of the roof. From its Gothic belfry the bell is said to toll by itself to warn boats in danger. According to legend, long ago the French fleet was being pursued and the bell of St They rang out to guide the ships to safety; but when the enemy fleet followed a strong current appeared, dashing many of their boats on to the rocks and dispersing the rest out to sea.

St They's plain exterior gives no hint of its interior of ornate gilded columns and pillars and colourful plaster saints, one of them pointing to a nasty wound above his poor knee. This most maritime little church's turquoise arched wooden ceiling is reminiscent of an upturned boat; model boats stand in front of the two altars, and there's a lifebelt washed up from a shipwreck.

Cradled between the Pointe du Van and Pointe du Raz lies the Baie des Trépassés - the Bay of the Dead. Despite its forbidding name and macabre legends all to do with death, it's a glorious sandy beach where dead Druids were launched to the gateway to the other world on the Île de Sein. It's easy to see why they chose this as their final point of departure from the temporal world, because it would be difficult to find anywhere more naturally splendid. It's so beautiful that it hurts. In the 6th century Saint Guénolé built a bridge of ice to link the Île de Sein to the mainland. But the Devil walked over it and melted it with his hot little cloven feet. To this day there is no bridge, and the island can only be reached by sea.

Satiated with scenery, we go in search of lunch, following the coast until the village of Kérity. The 'le Doris' restaurant serves an excellent meal of succulent salmon with a generous selection of fresh vegetables, and not the customary uninspiring little castle of boiled rice that is so often plopped onto the plate. I'm addicted to watching people, and fascinated by an English couple at the next table. They nod to us when we arrive, and say "Hello." Then they eat their way through a five-course menu as if they are expecting to take an exam on it later. They savour each mouthful reverently, staring at it on their forks, inhaling its aroma, and smacking their lips; but during the entire meal they do not exchange a single word.

Afterwards we walk beside the bobbing flock of sailing boats in the small harbour, stopping to read a plaque on the wall:

'From this harbour, on 23 and 24 June 1940, in response to a call from General de Gaulle, our following compatriots sailed to England aboard

Notre Dame de Bon Conseil to join French forces, and fought on all seas and all fronts for the honour of France and her liberty.'

There are eight names listed, and we wonder how many had returned safely to Kérity after the war.

We pass a lady cyclist with a small dog perched in a basket on her handlebars. She waves to stall-holders selling lacework and hot dogs, and seabirds poke around in puddles on the rocky beach.

Something rather awful happened in Saint Guénolé, where we arrive in mid-afternoon. In October 1870 the wife and daughter of Finistère's *préfet*, together with a friend, were swept off the rocks and drowned at the place known as the Hell Hole, or the Victims' Rock. Whatever was the *préfet* doing allowing his wife and child to put themselves into such a perilous situation? It does make you wonder if he was fit for purpose. A superfluous notice warns that this is a dangerous place. Anybody can see that. Even on this calm day the waves are heaving and crashing violently on the rocks. There's a sturdy iron rail designed to prevent people falling into the sea. Unbelievably, incredibly, ankle-deep in swirling foam on a small, wet, round rock stands a fisherman. He seems oblivious to the waters churning round him and sometimes over him as he calmly casts his line. When a couple of young men climb out of a car and into wetsuits and prepare to plunge into the sinister waters I drag Terry away before he has any crazy ideas.

After the last few days of doddling around deserted beaches and dozy villages, Concarneau comes as a shock. The streets are crowded, traffic almost stationary, and in oven-like heat the all-pervasive odour from France's third largest fishing port wafts into Tinkerbelle through every crevice and cranny. There's a funfair and shoals of squealing children swimming and splashing each other in the bay. Tally is astonished by the sudden change in our environment and climbs on top of the fridge for a better view. We continue to Pont-Aven where we drive round in circles looking for somewhere to park, past art galleries featuring seascapes and nudes, and more seascapes and nudes, until I suspect it is because of the multitudes of nude paintings that we are driving around, and not because we are lost.

Luckily we find a breakers' yard in Pont-Aven where we might be able to find a replacement exhaust system to stifle Tinkerbelle's roars. Unluckily it closes just as we arrive at the gates. Never mind, we'll be back tomorrow.

By sheer chance and great good fortune we arrive at a small, pretty car park in a grove of trees just a few metres from the beach at nearby Port-Manec'h. A friendly French couple come over to tell us that campervans are allowed to park here overnight. They have been here four days, but are now leaving. We must be very careful, they warn, because two nights ago a gang of drunken youths had attacked them. No damage was done, *mais quand même* …..

On the beach two dozen blue and white bathing huts stand like sentry boxes in a row. A few of them seem tired and are leaning on their neighbours. There are a couple of yachts anchored in the aquamarine water. It's easy to imagine Gauguin and his friends at their easels here, catching their pipe smoke with the brims of their straw hats, and dabbing idly at their canvasses.

When the dogs have had a run I put a couple of salmon steaks in the oven, and Terry and I stroll along a footpath through a copse leading to a cumbersome stone building standing on a small headland. A lean, lanky man appears wearing a checked shirt and faded blue jeans halfway down his snake-thin hips. Large spectacles magnify his bright-blue eyes, and an unlit aromatic pipe juts from beneath a walrusy moustache.

What are we doing, he asks. Without waiting for a reply he offers us a glass of wine and some oysters. We haven't any money with us, and I don't eat oysters if I can possibly avoid them, so we decline politely. He introduces himself - his name is Hervé - and vanishes inside the building. When he returns he's carrying two glasses of wine, a fistful of oysters and a sharp knife with which he points us to a table. A deafening noise is blasting from the building - I think it's the Ride of the Valkyries playing at thunderous volume on a radio that isn't precisely tuned to the station. Hervé won't have a drink himself, but expertly stabs open an oyster and holds it out to me. I hide my reluctance behind a gracious mask, and gulp down the vile thing. Terry finishes the rest. Hervé and his pipe sit between us. Quite what he is talking about we aren't sure, because all his tales taper off before reaching their finale. He is much given to elbow digging and long meaningful stares whose meaning we cannot grasp, and all the while the Valkyries are galloping more frenziedly through the radio's static crackling.

I begin to worry about the salmon in the oven and make getting-up-to-go moves; but Hervé signals me with his sharp knife to sit down while he regales us with a story featuring Admiral Donitz, some English submarines, and the barbarity of the Ukrainian soldiers who'd massacred the Port-Manec'h locals.

"When the Resistance - you know about the Resistance, don't you?" he jabs me with his elbow, and I nod - "When the Resistance caught the Ukrainians, you know what they did to them?"

"Killed them? Shot them?"

He puts his wide blue eyes close to my face, and says slowly and clearly:

"They cut out their tongues and dug out their eyes, and filled the holes with wire netting!"

"Why?"

"And you know why oysters are so expensive in England, don't you?"

No, I don't. I'm still waiting to learn about the wire netting. At the same time Terry is trying to keep up with the conversation in his minimal French, while I fill in the parts he can't get, without really understanding them myself.

"Well, I'll tell you." Hervé stares silently at me for several minutes, and I stare back like a rabbit hypnotised by a snake. I am seriously worried in case the salmon catches fire and burns the van down with the dogs in it.

"You want some more oysters, don't you?"

No, I say, thank you very much, we really don't want any more oysters. I don't add that if I never ate another oyster for the rest of my life I'd be perfectly happy. We do not know what our

18

relationship with Hervé is, if we are his guests, or his customers and are going to be presented with a bill that we don't have the means to pay. Ignoring our refusal, he goes away and returns with another fistful of oysters and puts them in front of Terry, who raises his hands in a gesture that says "No thank you." Hervé pushes them at him forcefully. Terry opens and eats them.

Now Hervé wants to arm-wrestle with Terry.

"Well, what a pity we must leave," I say. "We have a long way to go."

This is of course untrue. Hervé is a delightful man, but I am worried that if he knows we are staying in the nearby car park he might spend all night, to the accompaniment of the furious Valkyries, telling us stories that don't end and we can't understand, and forcing upon us oysters I don't want and we don't have the wherewithal to pay for. We all stand up, and Hervé kisses me six times; Terry receives one kiss and another arm-wrestle. Hervé writes his and my name on a piece of paper, and gives me six more kisses. Terry asks him how we can pay for the oysters. Hervé casually indicates a battered box on his table, and Terry empties into it all the loose change from his pocket, which didn't amount to very much at all.

We never learn why oysters are so cheap in France and so expensive in England, nor why the dead Ukrainians were filled with wire netting.

By the time we get back to Tinkerbelle the salmon steaks are almost but not quite beyond redemption. In the late evening we sit reading and watching a melange of blue tits, robins and chaffinches hoovering up the charred remains of our meal. A small green caterpillar humps itself ticklishly up my leg. The night passes peacefully; we are not attacked by intoxicated adolescents, but merely assailed by the pervading odour of burnt fish.

From now on, we agree, we will just have a cup of coffee in the morning rather than a proper breakfast, because by the time we've cooked, eaten, cleared up and organised the dogs in the back of the van half the morning has gone.

We set off early for the breaker's yard at Pont Aven to find an exhaust for Tinkerbelle. The industrial estate is strangely deserted.

The factories are all closed and the only sign of life comes from two noisy German shepherds hurling themselves at the fence. After several moments of bewilderment and indignation, we realise that today is the third of four public holidays in France during May this year. We rattle away to our next destination.

The countryside becomes tamer, more sophisticated; grander houses in tropical gardens replace the chocolate-box cottages of northern Brittany.

Morbihan

In Guidel the church bells are ringing merrily, the market is lively, and there's a show-jumping competition on the beach. Licking ice-creams, we watch horses bouncing over obstacles, and occasionally knocking them down like spillikins. Then we take the dogs to the beach where riders are cooling their sweating mounts. Seeing a creature similar in size to himself, Dobby joyfully bounds towards a horse and rider already teetering on the edge of control. The horse almost turns a somersault at the sight of the slathering black creature with a foot-long floppy tongue galloping towards it through the waves.

Next stop Lorient, where Terry is looking forward to visiting the submarine base, but there are no guided tours today because of the public holiday. However, a friendly young man at the gate says we are free to wander around and explore.

I find it a profoundly horrible place, a conglomeration of submarine pens, sinister concrete buildings with walls several yards thick. Even the few weeds struggling for life out of cracks in the concrete have a hopeless air. From here German U-boats crept out to attack Allied shipping in the Atlantic during the WWII. I break out in a sweat when I think of men locked inescapably in the ghastly vessels.

A single submarine sits at the dockside, a shiny black capsule reeking of stealth, death and claustrophobia. I want to escape from this awful place, but Terry is in his element, fascinated, ready to clamber into a submarine, submerge and sail off in it if he gets the chance. Then something else attracts his attention: a man working on a trimaran up on a trestle. He commands me to ask the man to invite him aboard, which I obediently do mentioning that Terry is an experienced ocean racer who navigated a winning British Admiral's Cup team yacht.

Soon Terry is up on deck with a charming and handsome Portuguese gentleman called Miguel, who speaks fluent English. He tells Terry the trimaran once belonged to France's greatest yachtsman, Eric Tabarly, who sadly fell overboard and disappeared at sea in 1998. Tabarly's boats were usually named Pen Duick, but this trimaran is called Côte d'Or II because she was sponsored by the chocolate manufacturers. She has an unfortunate history, having been dismasted and overturned twice. Miguel has rescued her and been working to rebuild her for the last year, whilst living in a container at the submarine base.

Terry is completely enraptured, while I'm stranded on the cracked and sweltering tarmac with the weeds and the horrible submarine, trying to keep the dogs cool. But soon I have a friend, a beautiful Spanish girl wearing a bikini and a huge smile, who rides up on a bicycle. Rosa speaks no English and little French, and I speak virtually no Spanish, but mostly due to her enthusiasm we find a common language. In between bouts of conversation she cycles round and round beside the boat, looking up at Miguel, and I think she's in love with him. She talks about him a great deal. He's her friend, and she comes from Spain to visit him several times a year. She stays at another friend's flat in Lorient. Miguel is in love with his boat, she says.

Rosa is outgoing: she tells me about her mother, who is from Asturia, and her father who is from Galicia. They're retired now and living in Asturia. She has a sister named Anjelica, who is a talented artist and is looking after Rosa's golden retriever while Rosa is visiting Miguel. Rosa comes from Corunna, a name that always takes me back to my schooldays when we giggled heartlessly as we recited 'The Burial of Sir John Moore after Corunna,' which at the time had seemed extraordinarily entertaining:

"We buried him darkly at dead of night,
The sods with our bayonets turning,
By the struggling moonbeam's misty light,
And the lanthorn dimly burning."

21

Since the Prestige oil tanker sank and flooded the Galician coast with twenty million gallons of oil, the local tourist industry is in decline, so Rosa is currently jobless. She doesn't mind, because she hates working in an office anyway.

Terry and Miguel are talking obsessively about sailing, and Rosa is cycling round in her bikini with her beautiful, tanned, slim body, gazing up at Miguel. She looks eighteen. She wants to take the dogs for a walk. She loves dogs, she says. We get them out of the van and they tow us around for fifteen minutes; then they're gasping so Rosa cycles off and brings back a bucket of water for them. I ask how old she is, and she astonishes me by replying that she's 33. I laugh and shake my head, and on a piece of paper write down 23? No, she laughs, writing down 33. Then she tells me about her boyfriend, who lives in Madrid and used to be an engineer, but now he has become an actor, which pleases her because it's a far more interesting career than engineering.

Is Miguel married, I ask tentatively, because he wears a wedding ring. Yes, she beams, his very beautiful wife is at home in Portugal, expecting their second baby in December. They're both very happy and she is happy for them.

She produces a digital camera and takes a photo of the two of us with our arms around each other. Finally I tear Terry away from Miguel and Côte d'Or II, and Rosa gives me a great hug, and I give her my bracelet. I'm totally charmed by this lovely girl who is content to spend weeks cycling around this strange area while Miguel works on his boat, her boyfriend is acting in Madrid, and Miguel and his wonderful wife are joyfully expecting another baby in Portugal.

Terry is very excited; he hopes Miguel will launch the boat in July. He has invited Terry to sail with him, possibly across the Atlantic. Mentally Terry is already packing his ditty bag.

The Quiberon peninsula is one long stationary stream of traffic stretching into the distance, so we head for Carnac to visit the church of St Cornely, patron saint of Carnac and horned animals. Also we want to see the ranks of megaliths said to be legions of soldiers petrified by Cornely to stop them chasing him. But there is no parking space to be had. Everybody and his wife are here today taking advantage of the unseasonably hot weather. We decide to go to Vannes for the night, via the Gulf of Morbihan, where the inland sea, says legend, was created by the tears of the fairies driven from Merlin's enchanted forest, Brocéliande. They tossed into it garlands of flowers which became the islands of Houat, the duck, Hoédic, the duckling, and Belle-Île, the Isle of Beauty.

The largest island in the gulf is the Île aux Moines (Monks' Island), half a mile from the second largest, the Île d'Arz (Bear Island). According to local legend (Brittany is very strong on legends!) the two islets were once linked by a narrow causeway, but the two communities hated each other. One were sailors who considered themselves superior to the others who were mere fishermen. When a boy from the Île aux Moines fell in love with a girl from the Île d'Arz, his parents imprisoned him with the monks. Every day the lovesick Arz girl crossed the causeway to sing beneath the walls of the monastery. The girl was so beautiful that she literally took away the breath from the inhabitants of the Île aux Moines. Believing this the Devil's work, the Prior called upon God's help. His prayer was answered: the sea rose and submerged the causeway. The girl was drowned and the two isles were separated for ever. Most of the legends in Brittany seem to end tragically.

Vannes has some sensationally pretty timbered buildings and a quaint old-fashioned cinema with a fading fascia bedecked with plaster roses. While the municipal campsite has a spacious lawned area for tents and caravans, campervans are restricted to a bleak and crowded tarmac patch. Our neighbours are a friendly Dutch couple who kindly lend Terry a bike so he can pedal to the nearest shop to buy something for us to eat.

I greatly admire the Dutch lady. She is strong-willed, and knows exactly what she does and does not like. She most particularly doesn't like cooking, so she doesn't cook. Ever. No ifs. No buts. Fortunately her partner loves cooking, so while she sits and relaxes he happily takes care of the catering department. When I raise the subject with Terry he just grunts.

Next morning we stop to let the dogs run at an unusually unpleasant beach of pebbles and coarse sand. Several giant beige-tinted jellyfish lie dead upon the beach, like transparent bowler hats. Dobby tries to eat one, but its size and resilient texture defeat him. After a while he gives up and joins Tally who is making inroads into a dead seagull.

For our breakfast we go to the historic Viking town of la Roche-Bernard in the Vilaine estuary. In the quiet square a life-sized silhouette of a kneeling man awaits the guillotine blade that will decapitate him. It's a reminder of the bloody Vendée rebellion when the revolting peasants and Chouans engaged in civil war against the Republicans. Nowadays la Roche-Bernard is a peaceful and lovely small town of cobbled streets, medieval buildings with brightly coloured shutters, and stone walls sprouting clumps of poppies and wild flowers. A most pleasant place to visit on a summery morning. Yachts relax in orderly ranks in the river, overlooked by two rusting cannons pointing at a row of beehives in a field of cornflowers. The guns are from the great 17th century warship La Couronne, a reminder that the town was once an important naval shipyard.

PAYS DE LA LOIRE
Loire-Atlantique

Oh Brittany, what a wonderful experience you have given us, with your magnificent scenery, beautiful towns, glorious food, intriguing legends and tropical weather. Will any other part of France delight us as much, I wonder?

Now we are in the Loire-Atlantique, once part of Brittany and still regarded as such by many Bretons, but currently engulfed into the Pays-de-la-Loire region.

Wobbly foals filled with *joie de vivre* totter behind their mothers through marshy fields of buttercups in the Brière Regional Natural Park. We are on our way to le Croisic where a brochure says there is a splendid aquarium with a restaurant where the food is served by divers. The aquarium closes for lunch just as we arrive, so we go directly to the restaurant. The waiters and waitresses are ordinary terrestrial creatures, and not divers at all. We'd visualized them swimming to the tables somehow bearing trays of food and drink without it getting wet or floating away. Terry is irritated and insists I ask the manageress where the aquatic servers are. She looks at me blankly and plainly hasn't the least idea what I am talking about. Terry is hungry and not at his normally good-natured best. He wants me to cross-examine the lady, and force her to produce waterborne staff; but I am already sufficiently embarrassed by the strange looks she is giving me, so I say if he wants to get involved in that kind of contretemps he'll have to speak French, and the misunderstanding is probably due to translation error.

Despite being served by earthlings, our meal is excellent. We have *moules* with *frites*, followed by salted caramel *crêpes*. The addition of a pinch of local salt does something very special to the caramel. We are washing it down with teacups of cider when suddenly the restaurant plunges into semi-darkness. There is much shouting and yelling, some laughter and a worried conversation. The power failure has knocked the credit-card payment machine out of action, and a person trying to pay for his meal claims to have no cash. The manageress has no intention of letting him escape without paying. After a few minutes he reluctantly admits that he has a chequebook, and settles up slightly sheepishly.

I am worried about the well-being of the fish if the electricity is going to be off for long, but our waiter says there is a generator for emergencies and the fish will be fine.

The aquarium opens as we finish eating. It is a fabulous underwater world of infant oysters and baby lobsters - quarrelsome characters with their claws bound to prevent them mauling each other; infinitesimal plankton and cute young sturgeon with tip-tilted noses. Herbaceous borders of sea anemones waft their tentacles dreamily at spider crabs and the fearsome-looking but harmless wolf fish. A spiny lumpsucker with Brigitte Bardot lips and big eyes mouths silent messages to us through the glass. Sunflower stars almost three feet in diameter cheerily wave their numerous limbs.

Crossing a walkway to visit the Australian sharks and manta rays, we are shocked to see into a room where white-coated people are busily chopping up fish. However, this is not a massacre of the inhabitants, but lunch for the penguins who are swimming around excitedly in their pool.

Gurnards line up in an orderly row too with their sad faces and funny legs all round their heads. Ethereal jellyfish float around in a glass cylinder. We read that they are related to sea anemones, composed of 90 per cent water, extremely fragile, with a short lifespan. Not much going for them, really.

A large spider crab stands upright rubbing together what look like little hands, like Uriah Heep, while odd things in its mouth move up and down like piano keys. Next to the yellow feathery corals are incubating spotted dogfish eggs, huge things like stag beetles; they undergo an eight-month incubation period and we can clearly see the embryos moving inside the casings. Seahorses prance and hook themselves to coral branches with their curly little tails, and everywhere it seems as if the fish are watching us as much as we are watching them.

As well as the exotic residents are the more mundane, those normally destined to end up coated in batter and surrounded by fried potatoes. It is only small swivelling eyes on the floor of a tank that betray the presence of flatfish-like turbot and plaice camouflaged in the sand. The iridescent shoals of mackerel twisting in a perfectly choreographed aquatic ballet are such sensitive souls, explains a notice, that they cannot survive longer than ten seconds out of water, or being touched. And all cuckoo wrasse are born female, and pink, but as they mature some of them change into males, and turn blue! "Pink for a little girl, blue for a boy," in the words of the song. Amazing. *Le Croisic* aquarium is every bit as wonderful as it claims to be. It might be a while before we can eat fish without feeling uneasy.

We are going to Guérande next. Over the last twenty years a new generation of *paludiers* has been working to revitalise the industry for which the town was once renowned - salt. Alongside the road, workers use traditional wooden rakes to scrape the grey crust from the salt pans. The town is busy with holidaymakers flocking to the gift shops to buy bags of damp, coarse grey salt, or the finer and more expensive pure white "flowers of salt." We take the dogs for a walk through the walled medieval town. Tally spots a cat in an alley and catching Terry unawares almost jerks him off his feet as he tries to follow it. A cluster of camera-laden Japanese tourists scatter in panic.

After buying a small linen bag of salt to support the local industry, we splutter along in Tinkerbelle to the fine beach at Pornichet. Tally, whose manners are normally as impeccable as his breeding, runs down the sands to where a couple are peacefully relaxing. The man lies on his stomach, propped up on his elbows reading a newspaper. Beside him his wife is on her back soaking up the sun. Tally stops three feet from the newspaper-reading man's elbow, adopts an unmistakable posture, and proceeds to defecate copiously. There is only one thing I feel I can decently do, and that is to walk in the opposite direction acting as if Tally is nothing to do with me. From a safe distance I see Terry assess the situation. As he talks to the man I watch their body language to see how difficult the man is going to be. He hands Terry a sheet from his newspaper, and stands up. While Terry makes a neat parcel, the man makes a fuss of Tally. When Dobby joins the party the sunbathing lady plays with him and I feel it is safe to venture over and join them.

They breed German pointers, and declare they have fallen in love with both our dogs. Although Tally is the aristocrat and Dobby of unknown origins, it's usually Dobby who attracts the most attention. He is a very handsome animal, and people frequently ask what breed he is. I once heard Terry describing him as a *'braque noir'*, translating as a black pointer. Tally is what the French call a *'braque hongrois'* - a Hungarian Vizsla. I tell people that Dobby is a *'chien de carton'* - a cardboard box dog because he was found in one.

Our new friends keep stroking the two dogs and saying how beautiful they are, which is quite true. They are beautiful dogs. While we are talking and watching them play, Dobby runs back and urinates for what seems like eternity all over the lady's white fluffy beach towel. Mortification just doesn't describe how we feel, but they laugh and recall situations where their dogs had similarly embarrassed them. They send their daughter and her boyfriend back to their house - a few yards from the beach - to bring their own dogs out to play. While they chase each other into the sea, the man tells us he is a journalist on the local newspaper. They have spent the day on a replica sailing ship which is departing from Saint-Nazaire this evening. If we watch the headland we'll see it passing.

He urges us not to park in isolated places for the night; the days are gone when it was safe to do so. These are dangerous times: this morning the body of a young boy abducted some time previously was found in a lake in Guérande.

We drive on to the harbour at Saint-Nazaire, where a three-masted square-rigger named the Stadt Amsterdam is preparing to sail. People scramble about on her decks amid a jungle of ropes and blocks; they climb rope ladders and edge out on to the spars of her masts like circus performers, loosening the sails. The Dutch ensign flies from her stern, and a courtesy French tricolour from her standing rigging. Both flags are comprised of red, white and blue stripes; sailors say you can tell which is which because the Dutch do it lying down, and the French standing up. There is a small crowd watching, a dozen people at most, the men all enthralled and the women visibly bored and cold as the sun goes down and a nippy wind springs up.

"I hope they sail her out," says Terry, "and don't use her engine."

We wait in the wind, and the ship waits for the wind. We wait, and she waits, until the tide had risen to the level of the water in the harbour and the lock gates open.

Terry is spellbound as the upper and lower topsails on her foremast and main mast unfurl and are sheeted in to trap the wind. Slowly gathering momentum, she glides out into the Atlantic Ocean towards the sunset, driven only by the wind. It's a scene from the romantic age of sail.

After the ship has disappeared into the distance we drive down to the docks to enjoy la Nuit des Docks. This is Saint-Nazaire's rather original idea of using clever lighting focused on various structures around the dockland to bring it to life at night. As dusk falls the lights came on; giant gantries and cranes twinkle, and the warehouse walls glow green and red, the lights reflecting in the black waters. The coloured spectrums change slowly, subtly, and more buildings emerge into the scene. By the time we leave the whole docklands have been transformed into a Technicolor post-apocalyptic scene.

It's late and we have no idea where to stay. Had we not met the journalist this afternoon we might have found a deserted place at the back of the docks for the night. We decide to heed his warning and drive until we find a car park opposite the Mairie at strangely-named Saint-Michel-Chef-Chef. The campervans have barely sufficient room between them to open the doors, but we squeeze in. It might not be very inviting, but it is at least safe.

Early next morning a wedding party arrives. The bride is magnificent, like a galleon in full sail, enormous but pretty, with pearls in her hair and a full-length billowing white satin dress trimmed with pink rosebuds. Her bridegroom is thin and looks bewildered. All their friends' cars are decorated with net posies and ribbons flying from their aerials, a tradition in France. Later they'll all drive in convoy hooting loudly in celebration.

Terry asks me to go and talk to the owner of a nearby campervan similar to Tinkerbelle, to ask if he has problems with his gearbox. Tinkerbelle's gear lever has started flopping around limply. The man is talkative and friendly with a pencil-thin moustache and a worried-looking wife. I explain about Tinkerbelle's loose gear lever. He puts a hand on my arm, and in a sympathetic tone says that our gearbox is totally *foutou* – a French word that translates into English with varying degrees of vulgarity, but the bottom line means that it's had it. It's the worst possible thing to happen, he says, because it's impossible to repair and, worse still, impossible to find a replacement part. Very soon our gearbox will fail completely, just as his did in Angoulême last year. He asks his wife to corroborate the unfortunate episode. She nods briefly and looks away. Oh! what a horrible experience they'd had, he remembers: they had to abandon their vehicle and at hideous expense hire a car to get home to Saint-Nazaire. Then there was the exhausting hunt for a replacement; but nobody manufactures parts for these vehicles any more. He estimates we have perilously little time left before our gearbox gives up the ghost entirely. It is our *pignon baladeur* that has gone; he hopes we don't have far to go, because he very much doubts we'll get there. I listen in terrible dismay, translating to Terry and envisioning us stranded on the road hundreds of miles from home, with no *pignon baladeur*, two dogs and several thousand miles still to travel. Terry is frustrated because I don't know how to translate a *pignon baladeur* and anyway, he asks, how does the man know what the problem is if he hasn't even looked at Tinkerbelle's gearbox? I don't know, I say, all I'm doing is trying to translate.

The little man watches us with crafty eyes, and throws us a lifeline. It is our lucky day, because when he'd managed, at unspeakable cost and with unimaginable difficulty to locate the part for his own van, he'd bought not one, but two. The other, which was by far the better of the two and virtually new, is in his garage at this very moment, not twelve miles from where we stand. As you might guess, something of such rarity is worth a fortune, almost as much in fact as we paid for all of Tinkerbelle. His wife shuffles and looks anywhere but at us. We thank him and tell him it is too expensive and we will take our chances with our foutou gearbox. He shrugs, says "*Comme vous voulez,*" (It's up to you), climbs into his cab and drives away.

"Add a *pignon baladeur* to the list," says Terry, "and when we find a breaker's yard, we'll get one there."

To add to the anxiety of Tinkerbelle's thundering exhaust, suspect brakes and temperamental clutch I add the fear that our adventure will be wrecked by whatever the pignon baladeur is.

The landscape on the Atlantic coast is flatter, and more open than Brittany. Bright white bungalows with blue shutters and pantiles take the place of stone cottages and slate roofs, and little coves become long straight beaches. Intermittent disused gun emplacements squat along the coast, an ugly reminder of the past. People dig in the seaweed-carpeted beach, poking things out of the sand. A chap wades into the sea in a wetsuit, while a couple paddle past in a canoe that looks about to sink. Two small boys pedal demonically through the traffic. It's the seaside in full swing.

Vendée

Skirting the Baie de Bourgneuf, where herds of fat ponies graze the salt marshes, we cross into the Vendée and the Marais Breton. The road leads through the muddy oyster- and mussel-producing port of le Collet, a flat area trembling in a violent easterly wind that whistles and wails through the masts of the boats in the harbour.

Tally has developed a proprietorial attitude regarding Tinkerbelle. He protests loudly, somewhat hysterically if cyclists, pedestrians or other dogs come anywhere near. Dobby tilts his head in puzzlement, unsure whether he should bark.

At Beauvoir-sur-Mer we follow a sign to *la Maison de l'Âne* (The House of the Donkey). Some fifty donkeys, mules and horses live here with a collection of assorted poultry. They're the children of a dark, handsome man called Paulo Dieumegard. When we arrive Paulo is perched on a three-legged stool in a cosy barn, milking a placid donkey mare into a plastic jug. Her foal is running up and down the next-door stall, yelling that his lunch is being stolen. Paulo assures us that the mares are only milked once a week, so their babies aren't deprived of their natural food. Donkey or asses' milk is pure white with a firm frothy head any beer could be proud of. It tastes, Paulo says, similar to coconut milk, and is rich in vitamins and minerals. Ideal for people with skin problems, but no good for making butter or cheese because it has a very low fat content. However, it makes an excellent soap and is a far more practical way of keeping the complexion up to scratch than trying to wallow about in a bathful like Cleopatra. And cheaper, too: asses' milk sells for something like £12 a pint.

Paulo's passion is for saving rare breeds on the verge of extinction. We walk around meeting different breeds of donkeys and petting their furry, fluffy foals with spindly legs and tiny jewel-like hooves, ears that are far too big and velvety muzzles that explore our fingers and clothing. The animals are clearly well-loved and cared for and in radiant good health. Paolo likes to feed his animals organically, and tells us they thrive on the coarse grass of the salty marshes. La Maison de l'Âne is not a commercial venture but a labour of true love. We buy a bar of lavender-scented asses' milk soap for Vivien who, every time I phone her is either cooking a meal for friends, bathing and grooming one of the animals, redesigning the garden or retiling a roof.

As it's low tide we are able to drive over the causeway and on to the Île de Noirmoutier. The roads are lined with stalls selling oysters, mussels and locally-produced sea salt, and almost every inch of the seven-mile causeway is filled with parked cars and dry seaweed. Gulls and egrets share the vast expanse of sand with scores of wellie-wearing people armed with buckets and plastic bags, all prodding around in the small pools of water to excavate the shellfish lurking there. Frequent signs warn of the danger of drowning when the tide comes in, but the sea is invisible, withdrawn to beyond the horizon. It's difficult to imagine how quickly it can cover the sands and the causeway. With no vehicles in sight, it's a seaside scene from an earlier century.

Our overnight stop is at Saint-Jean-de-Monts, a resort with a magnificent golden sandy beach, long seafront and wall-to-wall modern low-rise apartment blocks. A couple of hundred yards from the beach is the area allocated for campervans. It's cramped, with about 18" between each vehicle, and the campers already there are doing their utmost to discourage newcomers. One girl flails her arms around shouting *"C'est complet."* (It's full). Terry manages to squeeze past her and into a narrow slot, leaving just sufficient space for us to get in and out. It's not the most attractive place to spend an evening but it is free, and with Tinkerbelle critically in need of new parts we must make sacrifices where we can to establish the contingency fund we hadn't allowed for.

At sparrows' crack we're on the beach, which is raked by a bitter wind and empty apart from a scattering of vacant mussel and razor clam shells, and two more of the giant jellyfish. Dobby retrieves a dead seagull from the surf and runs around joyously with it. He stares reproachfully when Terry says he cannot bring it into the van and play with it on our bed.

Even this early in the morning there's heavy traffic on the Corniche. This is such a different world from the unspoilt wildness of Brittany. It is full of new houses and buildings, highly developed and geared for mass tourism, filled with camp sites, playgrounds, quad-biking parks, giant slides and pizza stands, and a mini-golf park dominated by a giant green plastic frog, several plastic penguins, and three life-sized skewbald plastic cows. Most appealing is the family of coypus playing among yellow irises on the river banks; least appealing is a sign advertising a three-star campsite named Pong.

Paulo at *la Maison de l'Âne* had recommended a visit to somewhere called le *Potager Extraordinaire* (the Amazing Vegetable Garden) at la Mothe-Achard, a small town a short way inland from our course. Driving through the town we spot a completely naked blonde trollop sprawled in a blatantly, lewdly suggestive pose in the doorway of a café. We drive back round the square for a closer look, which reveals that she is a life-sized plastic model; an equally realistic pirate clambers from an upstairs window with a swag bag over his shoulder. Seems like a town with a sense of humour.

What is it that makes the Potager Extraordinaire amazing? Where can I begin?

Covering five acres is a collection of the most peculiar, intriguing and truly weird plants we've ever seen, felt, smelt or tasted, as the signs invite us to do. Gherkins explode when touched. There are plants that declare they smell of *crotte de chien* (dog poo). They do. We shan't be buying any seeds. There are tomatoes that look like sweet peppers; aubergines that look like tomatoes; other aubergines that looked like boiled eggs; mile-long beans; and gourds in the most astonishing variety of shapes and sizes, including one rather rude one used by Papuan males to shield Big Jim and the twins. Another is speckled, 7 ft. long and curled round like a coiled snake.

The colours of the vegetables and flowers are startlingly vibrant; purple stems and orange stems, hairy ones, smooth ones, shiny ones and spiky ones. Fruits are long and thin, round or flat. Chocolate cosmos smells like After Eight mints. There are plants with timid leaves that flinch and curl up tightly when touched, and two labyrinths, one of flowers, and one of corn. We all know the difference between a maze and a labyrinth, don't we?

In a sunny patch pumpkins relax and grow in preparation for the National Largest Pumpkin competition that takes place in October - the record stands at 780 lbs. The *Potager Extraordinaire* is indisputably the most fascinating garden we've ever visited. There is something to surprise and delight children and adults, gardeners or not.

By lunchtime we are in la Tranche-sur-Mer at a pizza restaurant. The Monaco Formula 1 Grand Prix is just about to start on the television. Like us, the restaurant's two owners are great fans of the sport, and we're happy to sit and watch the start with them before we order. Once the race is under way Eric cooks us the most perfect pizza. He is an adorable person with a kind, gentle and rather sad face. He tells us he is sad because his girlfriend has to live in Mexico to look after her mother. Eric hopes to make enough money during the summer from his new pizza business to enable him to go to Mexico to visit her.

Extract from *Travels With Tinkerbelle - 6,000 Miles Around France In A Mechanical Wreck*

For links to Amazon Kindle USA, Amazon Kindle UK & Paperback sales pages please go to

http://blackbird-digitalbooks.com

and click on the book cover

2
BEST FOOT FORWARD
A 500-Mile Walk Through Hidden France

A touching and inspiring tale of the Texan pioneering spirit, English eccentricity, and two women old enough to know better.

JANUARY - Message posted to Internet:
"Free use of French farm house in Poitou-Charentes in return for caring for animals (horses, dogs, cat, parrots, geese, fish) for six weeks while owner walks across France."

Reply: *"You must be joking!"*

Reply: *"My wife and I are prepared to care for your animals. Please give your exact location in Provence, details of local sights, shopping facilities, festivals, and whether transport is provided."*

Reply: *"There is no mention of how much you are prepared to pay. I couldn't do it for nothing."*

Reply: *"Hi. I saw your message. I am a 16-year-old student studying French, and would like to spend some time in France during the summer to improve the language. I like all animals. Would I be able to bring some friends who also like animals and want to improve their French?"*

Reply: *"I am very sorry. Please disregard my earlier response. You are not in Provence, and my wife doesn't want to do it anyway. Good luck."*

Reply: *"I would be ready to look after up to three dogs, but definitely no cats as I am allergic. What is the local nightlife like?"*

Reply: *"I am interested in your ad. I am an American lady from San Antonio, Texas, have kept horses and bred dogs and would very much like to visit France. Hope to hear from you. Jennifer."*

"Hi Jennifer. Thanks for your reply. I am an English woman, living in France, who is going to walk from La Rochelle on the Atlantic coast of France to Lake Geneva, just across the French/Swiss border. I anticipate that this will take 6 weeks; however, it could be longer. My start date is 1st May. My house is undergoing renovation, and is primitive but fairly comfortable. To be honest, I think making this kind of arrangement with someone as far away as Texas, USA, would be rather difficult. I anticipated it would be someone from England, who is already familiar with France. But if you are still interested, let us talk some more."

Reply: *"Ticket booked. Arriving Paris 10.00 a.m. Thursday 23rd April. Jennifer."*

The Beginning

In an attempt to withstand the relentlessly penetrating cold of a French January, I had taken to marching briskly around the wintry

36

lanes and byways in my locality for several hours each day. This tended to be marginally warmer than staying in the house. But when you have started from and arrived at the same point for about the thirtieth time, you begin to feel that there may be more to life than going round in loops, and it was this that led me to decide to walk, instead, from one place to a completely different one. So I thought I would walk round the whole perimeter of the country, but once I looked at the map I could see it would take me a year. On the other hand the nearest coastal point west of home was La Rochelle, which, if you drew a straight line eastwards, lined up handily with Lake Geneva, only about four hundred miles away, a journey which I estimated should take about six weeks. It was not a project to undertake rashly, so I thought about it very carefully for twenty minutes before going to visit my friend and neighbour Gloria, to announce my intentions,

"Guess what, I'm going to walk across France."

Gloria liked to get straight to the point. "When?" she asked.

"1st May. The weather will be just right then."

"Good for you," she replied.

And that was it, really. I started planning. It couldn't require anything more than a bit of commonsense, I thought.

There were a few potential snags—I'd never hiked anywhere further than a three-mile radius from my house before, nor pitched a tent; I didn't and never would understand how to use a compass; and my level of physical fitness was somewhere on a par with Mother Theresa and the Pope. However, by far the largest obstacle to the venture were the animals: two elderly mares, six dogs, a cat, two parrots, some fish and a pair of killer geese, who were going to need someone to take care of them while I was away. My husband Terry couldn't possibly leave his business unattended in England for several weeks; and, well, as a matter of fact, I hadn't actually mentioned the project to him. I knew perfectly well that if he learned about it in the early planning stages, it was absolutely certain that he would have succeeded in talking me out of going, as he is a great deal more sensible than I am, and so all the arrangements had to be concreted before I told him what I was doing. Unless I could find someone crazy enough to come and caretake the menagerie, the whole project was not going to happen; so I posted a message to an Internet board and, to my astonishment, netted Jennifer. There was nothing to stop me now.

Over the next four months I rambled around with a backpack laden with dictionaries and encyclopaedias masquerading as clothes and a tent. I tried to put in between twelve and twenty miles a day of walking at a steady three miles an hour, and during daylight it all seemed simple. The boots and socks I had carefully chosen were supremely comfortable and I could walk effortlessly for several hours. But at night, in the dark, my sleepless mind wandered over all the potential problems ahead, and a little voice kept saying: "You can't possibly do this thing, you silly woman. Swallow your pride and admit it," while another voice assured me: "There's nothing to it, just a question of putting one foot in front of the other. You said you were going to, now get on and do it."

When I went to the station to collect Jennifer, the fact that she didn't arrive as scheduled came as no surprise. Seriously expecting a total stranger to travel from Texas into the French unknown was being rather optimistic, and I didn't know whether I was pleased to be off the hook, or disappointed. Another train was due in from Paris in a couple of hours, so I hung around for that, just in case. As the passengers disembarked I skinned my eyes for a lanky cowgirl, but there wasn't one. The human straggle tapered out into an emptiness, and as I turned with a resigned shrug to leave the platform the rattle of little wheels and some gasping drew my attention to the bottom of the stairs. The noises emanated from a short, wide figure clad in jeans and checked shirt, topped by a huge Stetson, with a backpack over her shoulders and dragging a wheeled suitcase behind her. I waved. Her anxious expression converted itself into a brilliant ear-to-ear grin; she plucked off the Stetson and jammed it on my head. "Oh brother, am I glad to see you! I was real worried when I missed the train in Paris – the flight from the States was late getting in. And then when I didn't see a lady in a *bay-ray* waiting on the platform, I thought I'd made a terrible mistake coming here!" I'd forgotten that I'd promised to wear a beret.

Over a couple of beers Jennifer took in the local scenery, and we started getting to know each other a little. You cannot meet this lady and not instantly adore her. She is necessarily built on generous lines, because she has an enormous heart that embraces every person, beast or plant. Two devilishly blue eyes sparkle from an unlined face that gives no hint that she is a grandmother, nor that she has survived numerous major health problems, including cancer involving radical surgery. She married at fifteen, and raised her three children single-handed. Amongst various jobs she had taken to earn her living, she had driven a giant bulldozer in a uranium mine. She radiates warmth and kindness, merriment and dependability. I was quite certain that my menagerie couldn't be in better hands than hers.

I introduced her to Tinkerbelle, my twenty-year-old Citroën 2CV, whose bodywork was mostly held together by patches of corrosion. Jennifer chuckled "Oh my, what a cute little car!" laughing as we bumped and lurched along the roads towards home.

When we reached our slightly less than half-restored farmhouse, I held my breath. Although I had written to give a good idea of the state of the property, I wondered whether she would be prepared for the reality, and most particularly the archaic electrical supply, which was composed of numbers of extension leads plugged into each other and snaking their way from room to room, all emanating from a single ancient socket in one wall. "Oh gee!" Jennifer breathed, gazing at the crumbly stone and flint walls with pieces missing, and the sagging floors. "Just look at this. This is *real* history. We think the Alamo is old, but this is really something else." She constantly delighted in everything French—the countryside, the kindness of the people, the food, and the buildings. Everything thrilled her.

We'd agreed to spend a week together before my departure, to give her plenty of time to learn her way around the neighbourhood and the little eccentricities of Tinkerbelle, our animals and neighbours. We visited the local stores and introduced her to English neighbours and friends, so that she wouldn't find herself completely alone once I'd left.

The animals, with the possible exception of the geese, fell instantly under the spell of her soft American voice and gentle, firm approach, and I had no qualms about entrusting them to her care. Bill, my next door neighbour ran a business moving furniture for people between England and Spain, and his home here was a convenient half-way point for stopping off. However, he was currently in a French prison because a substantial haul of cannabis had been found on a vehicle belonging to him. I wasn't at all sure how Jennifer would react when I told her, but she was quite unruffled, and had soon added Bill's wife, Gloria, to the large brood already under her expansive wing.

What made her decision to come to France particularly valiant was the fact that only a few weeks before her departure from the United States, her father had become seriously ill. Following much heart-searching, and with the unreserved encouragement of her family, she had decided to go ahead with the venture, and to stay here for as long as it took for me to cross the country to Lake Geneva. Her arrival in a country she knew nothing of, with a language she could not speak, undertaking to spend several weeks in primitive conditions taking responsibility for twenty assorted animals was breathtakingly heroic.

Once she was comfortably and confidently established, I told Terry about the project, and despite his initial expostulations, once he had met Jennifer he conceded graciously to my mad whim, whilst telling me I was absolutely crazy and that he would be worried out of his mind while I was away.

"Don't be silly," I said breezily, "I've planned this quite meticulously and know exactly what I'm doing. Nothing can possibly go wrong."

An essential factor to the enjoyment and successful outcome of my journey was the weather, which had to be not too cold, because I hate the cold, and equally important not too hot because I keel over at anything much above 70° Fahrenheit. Having estimated the journey would take six weeks, by departing on 1st May when the weather would, I believed, have settled to a pleasant dry mildness, I would, I believed too, reach Lake Geneva before the blistering heat of summer.

And so it came to pass that I stood damp and shivering on the cobblestoned quayside of La Rochelle in the bay of Biscay, in a shroud of persistent drizzle driven by an Arctic wind, weighed down with a backpack I could hardly lift and looking at a journey of more than four hundred miles across terrain I knew almost nothing about, wishing that I was somewhere else, almost anywhere else. I wished too that I had kept my mouth closed back on that cold January day, and that someone would dissuade me, at this late stage, from my self-imposed madness; I would resist at first, protest a little, but gradually allow commonsense to prevail, and with an outward reluctance hiding an internal whoop of relief, would heft the backpack into the car and go home.

Nobody would be surprised—I knew that most people didn't believe I could or would do what I had said. And that was the main factor that drove me onwards—that, and the fact nobody made any effort to talk me out of it.

There weren't many people in La Rochelle that morning of 1st May, a public holiday marking the ancient pagan celebration of the start of summer, and the modern day recognition of the struggle for working class rights. It is traditional in France, on this day, to offer friends posies of lily of the valley, and the flower vendors hunched over their loaded handcarts on the chilled street corners. The narrow lanes were bordered by splendid mansions, embellished with outlandish gargoyles of dolphins, lions and griffins, and the 15th century timbered houses that were once the homes of wealthy merchants. La Rochelle had grown from a small fishing village in the 11th century to become one of the premier ports on the Atlantic coast. It was a rebellious and independent town that minted its own coins and raised its own army, and when Protestantism was born in the early 16th century, the people of La Rochelle embraced the new religion, which promoted a freedom of thought and deed quite different from the strict demands of the Roman Catholic Church. The town became a haven for the Huguenot Protestants, and an ally of France's great enemy, England. In the 17th century La Rochelle's power and independence was a thorn in the malevolent flesh of Catherine de Medici, regent of France, and the town had to be brought to heel. Besieged by land and sea by Cardinal Richelieu and cut off from any outside aid, over a period of several months 23,000 of the original 28,000 inhabitants starved to death. The survivors surrendered.

A blend of history and high-tech, today La Rochelle is the Atlantic home of the super-yachts, with a harbour depth that can accommodate a draught of up to sixteen feet and hosts major national and international nautical events throughout the year. The town has pioneered the use of electric vehicles; distinctive little yellow cars, and scooters, are available for daily hire; the urban dustcarts and ferries are electrically driven. The fishing industry thrives, as does heavy industry manufacturing amongst other things the high-speed TGV trains. It is one of France's largest tourist destinations and with its dozens of theatres and music festivals, a cultural centre par excellence. Restaurants abound in the streets of the old town and around the harbour. There are several museums, a magnificent aquarium, and one of the sunniest climates in the country.

From this harbour, protected for more than six centuries by the great towers of La Chaine and St Nicolas, pirates and merchants had sailed away. Explorers ancient and modern had left from here to find Asia, Africa and the New World in their quests for adventure, wealth and knowledge. The seamen of La Rochelle were famed for their bravery and expertise: *"They brave the seas, control the storms and, despite all the anger that the winds can muster, they sail beyond the Sun"* (Gaufreteau). Every one of them differed from me in one respect. They had all headed west. But then they had ships. If you don't, you've got to go east or drown, especially carrying a backpack and wearing heavy boots.

A few soggy tourists were braving the unspeakable weather in a spirited attempt to enjoy themselves, and behind a muffled loudhailer groups of chanting trades unionists, Communists and miscellaneous protesters trudged damply, half-heartedly waving droopy flags. Terry, Jennifer and Gloria had come to see me off, and my friend Carole, who planned on meeting up with me five weeks later so we could cross the Jura mountain range together. They all transparently thought I was quite mad, but after two

42

hours of drinking coffee none of them had tried to change my mind and I knew there was no way out. We walked past the yachts that swayed and clinked amongst a flotilla of mysteriously dead fish, and I didn't push either of Carole's frightful little boys in. I'd have quite liked to; I was allergic to them—they made my hands itch every time I saw them. Now they were becoming increasingly, unhappily vocal. It was a good moment to leave. You just cannot imagine what these kids were capable of when they were upset.

We hugged and kissed; Terry tightened my bootlaces and hoisted the backpack into place and Jennifer pressed into my hand a small brass box containing her lucky tiger-eye, which I stowed in my fanny pack with the camera and tape recorder. You might think with La Rochelle being such an important departure place for travellers to all corners of the globe that there would have been some indication of where to start looking for Geneva, but there wasn't. You had to work it out for yourself. There was a small canal pointing in an eastwards direction, so following Terry's advice I set off alongside it clenching a five-foot long wooden hiking stick in my fist, and a nine-inch folding knife in my pocket so that I could kill someone if I had to. Actually I carried three knives—one with a very sharp stabbing point, one with sharp serrations, and a jungle-camouflaged flick-knife that looked lethal and made a sinister hiss when opened, but was in fact little more than a glorified pen-knife.

After two hundred yards the canal vanished, just disappeared into nowhere. Suddenly, it simply wasn't there. I should have recognised that this was prophetic. I scrambled down an embankment and up the other side, arriving on a major road, where a bicycle drew alongside and a beaming black man with shoulder-length dreadlocks slowed his pace to mine.

"Where are you going?" he asked in French, in a melting chocolate voice.

"Geneva."

He wobbled slightly. "Geneva where?"

"Geneva in Switzerland."

"All alone? Like that? Walking all the way?"

43

"Yes, that's right."

"English?"

"Yes."

He shook his head and peeled away with a "Bon courage!" (Good luck – you're going to need it!) and, rather disconcertingly, I could hear him laughing wildly as he vanished into the distance.

For the next couple of hours I wandered around in the immaculately clean and tidy industrial zone trying to work out where I was, with not a lot of success. It was by luck that eventually I found a place that was marked on the map, a neat residential area not too far off-track from where I was meant to be. There was an unfamiliar niggle on my right little toe that needed to be investigated, so I sat down on a convenient stone bench. Apart from reaching Lake Geneva, my other target was to transform my unsatisfactory physical shape into something more like Elle McPherson, by dint of massive exercise coupled with spartan meals. In the backpack was an assortment of high-energy cereal bars and dried fruit—enough, I had planned, for six nutritious non-fattening breakfasts or mid-day meals. Many of the pre-packaged meals manufactured for hikers were meat-based. There wasn't a very exciting choice for someone like myself, a vegetarian who eats a little fish. The French still being a predominantly carnivorous race, shopping is never easy for a vegetarian on the move, and normally means bread, cheese, cakes and fruit, with which, in a tent and on a small single-burner stove, you are somewhat limited as to novel ideas.

After I had satisfied a deeply hollow feeling between my neck and my legs, there was just enough left for two meals if I ate sparingly. The niggly toe was bad news—it had a raw red patch with peely skin over it, something it had never done before. Why today, I wondered? Why now? I slapped a plaster on and set off again for my first destination, St Christophe.

Not long afterwards I found myself walking along a busy main road, instead of the quiet footpath which, despite being well marked on the map, didn't seem to exist. There was a very narrow strip of grass beside the road, and it looked pretty scattered with daisies, 19 buttercups, dandelions already turned to fairy colonies, bluebells and cowslips, cow parsley still green, and purple vetch all struggling not to get onto the tarmac and be crushed. It was just their bad luck that I came along in the gigantic hiking boots, because I am pretty certain that very few people had ever been stupid or misguided enough to walk on the side of this particular road. Fast, heavy holiday traffic driven with what the drivers probably thought of as panache, but which anybody else would regard as homicidal mania, compelled me to leap sideways into the knee-high grass to avoid becoming a road accident every time a vehicle passed. It wasn't terribly easy leaping about with the load strapped to my back, especially trying at the same time not to jump on the poor flowers. Passing motorists watched me curiously.

Whether there is anything of historical or other importance about St Christophe, I do not know—I hadn't been able to find a single fact about it in any guidebook or the entire worldwide web. It is a small and well-kept village of approximately nine hundred inhabitants, with a fine campsite that was my reason for being there. It was indeed the only village with a currently open campsite that I could reach within a day's walk of La Rochelle, although walking was not what I was doing by the time I arrived. Both feet felt as if they had come fresh from a session with the world bastinado champion; the backpack weighed four times what it had when I set off, despite most of the food it had held having been eaten, and my right hip was emitting a rhythmic clicking-grating sound. Walk? I could barely stand. The last four miles had taken nearly three hours to cover, as I limped, clicked, shuffled, sat on tree stumps, and constantly adjusted the backpack straps in a hopeless bid to make it lighter.

The exquisite delight of unstrapping the pack, and holding it for a moment longer than necessary, savouring the anticipation of dropping it to the ground, and the supreme joy of unlacing and removing the boots is something which I will remember for the rest of my life. From the lake beside the campsite a couple of dozen men, women and children engaged in a fishing contest watched as I shook the tent from its cocoon. I slid the single telescopic fibreglass pole into the channel designed for the

45

purpose and pushed the six metal pegs through the loops of the tent and into the soft mown lawn of the camping area, as nonchalantly as if it were something I had done for years, and not just once before, on the living room floor. After admiring my new home I hobbled over the grass in my socks to the bar where a trio of three knitting ladies sat clacking and chattering. They asked where I was heading for, and shook their collective heads in puzzlement when I said Lake Geneva.

"Where is that exactly?" asked one.

"It's in Switzerland," I said.

"Geneva! You mean *Geneva*?"

I nodded.

"Oh la la!" they cried. *"Oh la la!"* and standing in unison they waved wildly to a large figure across the lake, who detached himself from his fishing line and with a film-star smile of perfect white and gold teeth, and an outstretched hand introduced himself as the mayor of St Christophe. Was the campsite to my liking, he was kind enough to ask. Looking at the velvet lawns, immaculately symmetrical hedges and spotless sanitary block, I couldn't fault it, other than that it was totally bereft of any other campers. During the planning stages of this safari I had imagined arriving at campsites and finding them full, and had devised contingency plans (bursting into tears, collapsing, throwing myself on the mercy of other campers). He asked about my plans and nodded solemnly as I explained I would be leaving in the morning en route to Geneva.

"Please enjoy your stay. There is no charge. Let me know if you need anything. My house is just there." He pointed to a rooftop. "I wish you a pleasant evening and a safe journey."

I bought a couple of chilled beers from the knitting ladies and crawled into the tent, where I lay for half an hour, listening to the songs of the wild birds, occasional shouts of the fishing contestants, and the despairing wail of a peacock from the grounds of a nearby house. But mostly I was enjoying the relief from the weight of the backpack and the torture of walking, while idly wondering why today had been so unlike all the previous days of training, when the weight hadn't been a problem and my feet hadn't hurt.

When I tried to sit up, I found I had developed the flexibility of a railway sleeper. It was like *rigor mortis*—nothing would bend. I could neither sit, nor kneel, nor roll over. Nothing moved but my hands and eyes, and like a paralysed insect I lay on my back wondering what to do next. Maybe if I shouted loud enough the knitting ladies would hear and come to the rescue? But how damned stupid I would look. Finally, by grasping the legs of my jeans and heaving and writhing frantically, I managed to pull myself upright, and after a series of laborious and intricate manoeuvres, like a metamorphosing pupa I emerged from the cocoon of the tent to take a blissful steamy shower.

Dinner came out of a vacuum-packed aluminium envelope which promised that if you half-filled it with boiling water it would transform itself into a delicious meal of pasta and vegetables. This was only partially true; it did transform itself into something, but delicious it was not. I reached for an open beer bottle and successfully sent it flying over the sleeping bag, floor and my scattered clothes, but by now I was too tired to care, so leaving it to disappear osmotically I slithered into the moist sleeping bag and settled down with a torch and book.

When dusk arrived, the frosted creamy orbs of the campsite lights came on and glowed comfortingly through the night. There was no sound at all. Apart from the weather, my feet, the weight of the backpack and navigational difficulties, for the first day things could have been worse. Not much, though. I wondered how Jennifer was adjusting to her new lifestyle. I found a pay phone, and gave her a call.

"How are you doing?" I asked.

"I'm doing just great. I have to tell you, when we watched you fading into the distance today, we were all thinking the same thing: Are you sure you want to do this?"

"I still want to do it. Today went really well," I lied. "Are the animals behaving?"

"Oh, they played around a bit. I went down the lane to bring the horses home. I had no trouble getting them back to the paddock but when I got there Leila spooked and scared Cindy, and she took off running with her halter and rope still attached. Every time I got close to Cindy, Leila would take off again and Cindy would be right behind her. I did finally get them both in a corner and Cindy stepped on her rope. I had just taken her rope off when the two geese came charging after me."

"Well, it sounds as if they're testing you. I hope they don't give you too much grief. I'll call you tomorrow, and see you again in a few days."

"Take care now."

How Do You Say "Merde" In English?

The night was very cold and the ground was very hard and these conditions were not conducive to a good night's sleep. In the darkness the tent felt strangely clammy and wet, and as daylight arrived I could see a hundred rivulets of condensation racing each other in wiggly tracks down the walls, to join their predecessors and the remains of the beer in puddles on the floor, from where they seeped into my scattered belongings. My hair was wet. So were the too-thin mattress and far-too-thin sleeping bag. Outside it was a cold, damp and grey day exactly like the thirty-three which had gone before, so I swathed myself in a woolly vest, two T-shirts, sweatshirt and jeans, none of which were quite dry. While waiting for the water to boil for a cup of coffee, I draped my fragrant wet clothing and sleeping bag optimistically over the hedge in the hope they would dry, and went to do some shopping.

In the centre of the village a sign on the corner of a building read *Bar/café/épicerie* (Bar/café/grocery). Inside, a man was polishing glasses behind a bar.

"Good morning. Do you sell food?" I asked.

"No, not here. You must go to the *épicerie*, just round the corner." He pointed to the door through which I had just come in.

I exited and went round the corner and in through another door which led to the area behind the bar. The same man was waiting there, still polishing glasses. There were tins of meat, jars of meat, fresh meat in slices, lumps and chunks, frozen meat and not a lot else apart from some large heavy tins of beans. Confident that there would be somewhere en route where I could buy some bread and cheese for lunch, however, I wasn't too worried. I bought a bag of peanuts and some stock cubes, out of politeness.

The clothing and sleeping bag were as dry as they were likely to get, so I pushed them into the backpack. They didn't want to fit, but I pushed them really hard. They had fitted yesterday. As I tugged the final zip closed, the tag came off in my hand

The sun displayed itself for microseconds between jagged cracks in the grey clouds, and emitted no warmth at all, and I set off with a slightly sour feeling towards the weather. It was now May 2nd, the date when my nextdoor neighbour always puts her geraniums out, because it is safe to do so, she says, as the fine weather has arrived. Well, it hadn't in St Christophe.

I left St Christophe at just after 11.00am, and by mid-day gnawing hunger pangs had joined the miscellaneous discomforts that re-manifested themselves once I began walking. There were no shops in the first two villages I passed, and in the third everything was closed for lunch by the time I arrived, so I sat on the stone steps of the Post Office, eating dried apricots and peanuts and watching, through a pair of tall wrought-iron gates leading to an elegant house, a handsome and substantial cockerel busily uprooting plants from a raised bed in the garden, under the disapproving eye of a peacock and a large pink rhododendron.

The gently undulating landscape of the Charente Maritime looks at its best in summer, when fields of gilded sunflowers stretch to the horizon, interrupted by bright green rows of vines. In today's overcast conditions the acres of oilseed rape and wheat didn't quite pull it off. My right hip and left foot had been joined in their misery by the second biggest toe on the right foot, while both little toes felt as if at each step they were being vigorously caressed by a cheese grater. The diversity of pains was a benefit, because by concentrating on one at a time it was possible to overlook the others, so I could choose between stabbing, biting, grating or throbbing pains, adding an interesting dimension to a journey that was otherwise quite unremarkable.

Briefly the sun came out, and coming upon a convenient strip of newly mown grass behind the stone wall of a farmhouse I pulled off my boots and socks, and lay relishing the temporary warmth. The farmer drove by on a tractor, waved a cheerful hand and came across to ask not why I was sprawled peculiarly on his lawn, but whether I thought it was going to rain. That was anybody's guess. It hadn't yet, but apart from a few blue smears, the skies were still grey and heavy. He lamented the fact that the continual rain of the previous month was threatening to ruin his wheat fields, and that unless he could spray within the next two days, he would lose his entire crop to disease. To spray, he must have forty-eight dry hours. We discussed the unpredictability of weather the world over, and I thought it polite to apologise for being on his lawn. No, he said, he was pleased to see I had made myself comfortable there, my load looked heavy, and was I going far? I said I was heading for Surgères, the next campsite, as I didn't particularly want to be either laughed at or disbelieved when I announced my final destination, because the way things were going so far, I was starting to have doubts about it myself. Well, he announced comfortingly, I didn't have too far to go, only about another eight miles. He watched as I reshod myself, and helped me into the backpack. Could he offer me a cup of coffee? I declined politely, and wondered whether in England a farmer would have been so welcoming of a stranger on his land. The French do not seem, in general, to share the Englishman's territoriality, but maybe that's because there is a lot more land to go round in France. When they ask "May I help you?" that's what they mean, and not "What the hell are you doing on my land?"

Across a still barren, lumpy chocolate-coloured field a solitary hare sprinted, its long ears flicking, and two pairs of partridges blundered out from a thorny hedgerow right in front of me, then turned tail in noisy panic and scuttled back in again.

By 5.00pm I had reached the outskirts of Surgères, from where signs indicated the campsite. By following them I found myself on a two-mile detour along the main road, ending at the entrance to the site, just five hundred yards from where I had begun to follow them in the first place. Every part of my body hurt. I had

had nothing to drink since the coffee six hours earlier, and was too weary to walk to town a quarter of a mile away, so gulped down two cups of tap water. Then I discovered that I had lost my tent pegs. I felt like bursting into tears.

The campsite was overrun with a large contingent of travellers in sumptuous caravans spouting a forest of television aerials, with separate units housing fully fitted kitchens with electric rotisseries and microwave ovens. A row of washing machines swished rhythmically next to the sanitary block. Like a tangled mass of giant spaghetti, thick electric cables criss-crossed the ground from the vans to the power points, and through the lacy curtains of the caravan windows rows of glass and china gleamed on shelves. The men, all rather short of stature, wore smart sports jackets and tapered black trousers leading to neat little feet in pointed shiny black shoes; they stood talking and laughing around a collection of prestige cars polished to a mirror finish. The women were quieter, hard-faced and worn, and most of them wore short tight skirts and baggy sweaters.

I found a space between the caravans, and a supply of twigs to use as tent pegs; they sank easily into the damp earth. A small, brown and determined child wearing pink pyjamas and giant gold and ruby earrings, with a lustrous mane of gleaming chestnut curls, and a top lip glistening from a runny nose, kept trying to uproot the twigs as I put them in. It wouldn't give up, and each time I prised a twig from its grubby stubborn fingers it would remove another one. I tried ineffectually to drive it away, hoping its mother wouldn't notice and take offence, because despite my selection of excellent knives I didn't feel fit or ready for a skirt-tucked-up fight around the campfire. Eventually a slightly larger child came and dragged it away by the seat of its pyjamas.

From the emergency rations I excavated and demolished another nasty meal of pasta and a strange chocolate and semolina dessert that was simultaneously gritty and mushy, and devoid of any taste. Instead of a cheese course I took four strong painkillers, and hoping the twig-pulling child would hold off for the night, zipped myself, fully dressed, into the sleeping bag.

There were four mallards on the tiny river Gères bordering the campsite; through the night the three drakes relentlessly pursued the single duck, and her indignant protests rattled in the dark. The wind rustled the trees and spots of rain fell. It was not warm in the tent.

Next morning dawned even colder and greyer than the previous day. The pink-pyjama child wandered around in the drizzle, resolutely resisting all attempts by assorted adults to feed it into an anorak, expressing its resistance by sitting down with a fierce thump and rubbing the offending garment into the mud. The travelling ladies seemed to spend all their time washing clothes, washing dishes or washing their caravans; they were all out in their nightclothes in the early morning, washing and polishing their immaculate homes despite the persistent gentle rain. I wondered whether they enjoyed their nomadic lifestyle quite as much as their little spouses.

A swirling wind kept tugging the flame from under my small gas stove, preventing the water from boiling. After a cup of lukewarm water with a brown scum floating on the surface, which I pretended was a cup of coffee, I decided to stay for the day and give my feet an opportunity to get their act together, and having by now eaten nearly all my food supplies, hobbled into town to restock. On the way back I stopped at a wine cellar near the campsite, where they sold wine from giant stainless steel tanks, through long hoses ending in a petrol-pump type dispenser. An old man slouched against the counter, with the sad, blurry eyes of a committed drinker, a purple face and a moustache that needed mowing. He grunted into a glass of red wine and I thought it wasn't often one saw quite such a disreputable person about in broad daylight, let alone before 10.00am. I bought a litre of sauvignon for twelve francs, and was walking back to the campsite when muffled shouts issued from behind. The committed drinker was shuffling unsteadily towards me, both arms flailing in the air, and I waited for him to catch up. When he did so he pressed a fifty franc note into my hand, stuttering through his moustache that I had dropped it in the cellar. As my total daily budget to cover campsite fees, food, phone calls and any other incidentals and emergencies was one hundred francs (twenty US dollars) I couldn't thank him sufficiently, and was humbled by my earlier judgement of him.

A large communal room at the campsite provided a comfortable and warm sanctuary from the hateful weather and would be a good place to write up my diary, so I installed myself, spread out my notes and map No. 2 (to see whether I could find a shorter route to where I wanted to go, which I couldn't), and settled down contentedly. About eight seconds later the door burst open and two little brown-skinned girls exploded into the room. The younger of the two, about nine years old, was very forward and either didn't know, or didn't care, about personal body space. She leant on the back of my chair, her bony brown elbow digging painfully into the side of my neck, while her companion watched her with admiration.

"What are you doing?" demanded the forward one.

"Writing." I jolted my shoulder so that the bony elbow lost contact.

"What are you writing? What is it about? Are you English? What are you doing here? Why don't you have a car? Please can you spare a few francs?"

I tried to be patient, answering all her questions, giving a negative response to her request. She shrugged good-naturedly.

A little brown hand closed over my map measurer—a small high-precision wheel that converted squiggles on maps into distances.

"What's this?"

I explained, and they insisted on being shown how the device worked, selecting random points on the maps which I had to measure. When I announced the distance, they gasped and asked suspiciously: "Are you *sure*?"

A small boy joined us.

"Go and get three pencils," their chief commanded me imperiously. "We are all going to play schools, and you can teach us how to write."

I wished they would go away and leave me alone.

"No. I don't have three pencils, I'm busy and I don't want to play schools. Why don't *you* be the teacher?" I suggested.

"OK". She flitted out of the door and returned a few moments later, with sheets of paper and pencils. Soon her two companions were bent over their work, obeying her barked orders.

I enjoyed ten minutes in peace, and then she was back.

"Teach us English," she ordered.

"Listen," I said. "I am trying to do something important. Please leave me alone."

She squinted at me for a moment, then offered peace terms.

"You teach us two English words, then you can do your writing."

I agreed, and had a good idea what the words were going to be. The three clustered around me, giggling expectantly, eyes bright.

"Go on. What's the first word?"

"Merde!" shouted the leader. I was right.

"Shit," I replied.

"Shit! Shit! Shit! Shit!" they chanted happily, clutching at each other in delight. I asked what the second word was, already knowing.

"Pi pi!" they yelled together. Right again.

Here lay a potential danger: in France Enid Blyton's famous children's character Noddy is known as *Oui Oui* (and Big Ears, his trusty companion, for some unfathomable reason, as *Potiron* (Pumpkin).

"Pee pee," I told them. "It's the same in English." If we got into semantics about wee wee, explanations would become impossibly complicated and I would never escape.

"Shit! Pee pee! Shit! Pee pee! Shit! Pee pee!" they trilled in unison, and rushed off to tell their friends.

Outside it drizzled with soft persistence. As an alternative to spending an afternoon being harassed by these merciless little people, there was no contest. Enveloped in a capacious red nylon poncho which would have accommodated a hippopotamus and left room to spare, I dashed from the campsite before they could see me.

In a bakery on the main road in Surgères the great wood ovens glowed and the proprietor shivered, remarking how cold it was. I wondered how he would feel in the tent. He announced comfortingly that the current weather would remain unchanged until 23rd May. Why this date precisely he couldn't explain, or possibly I couldn't understand, but it seemed to be something to do with local lore and was a depressing prospect.

The Sunday-afternoon streets were quiet and almost empty, and I wandered about steaming damply inside the poncho, admiring gardens that enfolded clumps of sad white lilies, sweet-smelling roses, honeysuckle, vivid geraniums and pansies and impossibly beautiful jungles of wisteria. I walked around the public gardens, through the Renaissance gate, around the ramparts of the 16th century château, which had been home to Hélène of Surgères, beautiful and gentle lady-in-waiting to the evil Catherine de Medici, and the 11th century church of Notre Dame de Surgères, ornately carved both within and without, an impressive example of that style of architecture known as Romanesque, for which the Poitou-Charentes region is famous. Below the ramparts a fledgling blackbird was flopping around perilously close to the road, so I ushered it back into the shelter of the shrubbery, while both parents bounced around and screeched indignantly as it clumsily flapped and hopped its way to safety.

Back at the campsite, the determined little travelling folk lay in wait. Like cats, they seemed to have an unerring instinct that drew them to those people who would most prefer to be left alone by them.

"You look like Little Red Riding Hood," said the bossy one.

Having seen my reflection in shop windows, I thought it was far more like Quasimodo playing Father Christmas, especially with my strange new gait. Not only was I festooned in the red poncho, which incorporated a shapeless baggy lump on its back to accommodate the backpack, but a completely rigid right hip forced me to walk stiff-legged, and to reduce the pressure on the ball of my left foot I tried to walk on the heel, toes pointed upwards. Not all the time though. The little toes of both feet were so sore that sometimes I walked on the inside edges of my boots to give them a rest. There was no doubt about it, it looked odd.

The little girls watched as I lit the gas stove and boiled some water to make a hot drink. However, closer examination of the stock cubes that I had politely purchased in St Christophe showed that they contained lard, so I gave them to the children, telling them to give the cubes to their mother. Some time later they returned and stood around sheepishly. Bossy pushed the more timid older girl forward.

"Please, Madame. How do you eat these?" She held out the mangled remains of a soggy cube.

I hid a smile and wished I had something nicer to give them. I asked whether they went to school.

"No," said the younger one rather sadly. "We're travellers, and we don't stay anywhere for long. Maybe one day ....." She trailed off. She told me they were of Spanish origin. They were bright and inquisitive and left to amuse themselves, and I wondered what their future would be.

Behind us, voices rose. A girl of about eighteen stood red-faced and tearful, glaring at three of the small-footed men who were talking quietly to her. Suddenly she turned and ran sobbing and wailing into a caravan, slamming the door behind her. The men shrugged, smiled at each other and wandered off. I thought what an experience it would be to share their nomadic lifestyle with these people, and to learn and understand their ways.

To have a shower at the campsite, you had to buy a token for ten francs. The *gardienne* (campsite warden) recommended the second shower on the right.

"You get a full ten minutes of really hot water in that one," she confided.

You did, too. It was absolute bliss.

I made a call to Jennifer. She'd been having fun getting used to driving my eccentric car, Tinkerbelle, whose peculiar gear lever made finding the correct gear something akin to solving a Rubik cube with your hands tied behind your back. She'd taken Gloria shopping; as she wrestled and wrenched, Gloria held on for dear life and they were both laughing tears. The gear lever wasn't

Tinkerbelle's only idiosyncrasy. She had no key to start her, as it had jammed itself in the lock one day, most inconveniently in a supermarket car park, and had to be drilled out of the lock. It had been replaced with a starter switch taped to the steering column. The horn was on a stick that looks like a turn signal indicator, and to open the window for air you pushed the bottom half of the window out to flip up and connect with the top. Sometimes it stayed up and sometimes it didn't.

She told me: "Your car is so much fun to drive, it's like being in 'Comedy Capers.' But what you call a two-way road here is about as wide as one lane of the streets we're accustomed to. When you meet an oncoming car there are only inches between the two cars. The other cars don't flinch and they don't move over. I find it really scary."

"Don't worry, you'll soon get used to it," I assured her cheerily.

The sauvignon, which was excellent, and of which I drank the lot, with a baguette, a chunk of rubbery cheese and four painkillers made a simple supper, and I settled down for the third night under the clammy nylon roof.

Following another arcticly cold night, I woke damp as usual, but my hip had stopped hurting. By misreading my watch, I gained an hour and after another cup of brown scum was on my way to Dampierre sur Boutonne, by 7.15am. The travellers were still sleeping.

Surgères seemed to be rather short on road signs, and I couldn't find any indication of which way I should be going. The compass wasn't any help—the needle kept spinning in a frantic, fruitless search for north, and even if it hadn't, I didn't have much idea how to use it. If I didn't know where I was, what help would it be knowing where north was? I had decided to rely on the sun for navigational purposes, because, impervious to damp and shock and regardless of magnetic interference it would still rise in the east and set in the west. As long as it was ahead during the first part of the morning, to my right for the middle part of the day and directly behind me in the early evening, I would be travelling in approximately the right direction, and when and if the thing ever came out again, it would be a great help. I'd been told that another way to work out direction was to see which side moss grows on a tree trunk, but the trees I examined had either no moss at all, or moss all round, so as far as direction went, it was down to guesswork.

After circumnavigating an industrial area, the railway station and a sprawling housing estate (twice), I took a major road because it looked as if it should go where I wanted it to. One and a half hours later, I was four and a half miles off route in a northerly direction. The shortest distance between Surgères and the next staging post on my route, Dampierre sur Boutonne, was twenty-one miles, and additional mileage was the last thing I needed. If I turned back it would add another nine miles to the day's journey making it impossible to reach Dampierre that night —and there was nowhere closer. A battered sign indicated a wine cellar and free tastings down a narrow lane, so that's where I headed for. Maybe 9.00 am was early to start on the bottle, but when in Rome .... - and I really needed somewhere to sit while I worked out a solution to my new predicament.

I followed the sign into a small village, where the entrance to the wine cellar was blocked by a yellow van. A postman's van. It was no less than a gift from Heaven, even better than a drink and certainly a lot more useful. Was it possible, I asked the postman, to cut across country to get back on course again, and so avoid a long trek back to where I had started? I flapped the map at him and pointed to Dampierre. He pursed his lips and shook his head. The area was a network of farm tracks and footpaths and almost completely devoid of signs. He didn't advise risking it, because he was certain I would get lost. I was sure he was right.

As he was going towards Dampierre, he offered to give me a lift, which I refused on the grounds that I was meant to be walking, and taking a lift would be cheating.

"Well, if I only take you to the point you would have reached if you had been going in the right direction, would that be all right?"

I couldn't see why not, nor think of any practical alternative, so we agreed a point on the map and he handed me gallantly into the back of the comfortably carpeted van, where I settled back to watch my new friend and saviour going about his daily business, which he did with great dash and style. We sped round the village, the van drawing up with no more than the width of a coat of paint between the walls of the narrow passageways, dropping mail nimbly into letterboxes positioned at exactly the right height to enable him to reach them without getting out of the van, or even stretching his arm.

I remarked how convenient this was for him.

"Yes," he replied. "My customers are very kind. They have all put their letter boxes in the best possible position to make my job easy."

How did they know how to do this?

"I told them," he explained. "And those people who couldn't put up the boxes themselves, I did it for them."

Out of a round of several hundred houses, only two required him to get out of his van. He was a lively and friendly man, who, once he finished his post round, spent his time renovating old houses and renting them out. He dropped me at the agreed spot, a short distance from the small village of St Félix, where in a loft above the corner shop, which smelt mustily of age and spices, a motherly lady served a warm buttery croissant and a perfect cup of coffee.

Fortified and relieved to be back on course, I tottered along the road, no longer stiff-hipped, but the soles of my feet were raw and burning, and the backpack gouged furrows into my shoulders. I kept adjusting my grip, sometimes dragging down on the loops attached to the shoulder straps, and sometimes jamming my arms through the straps and locking my fingers together. It didn't make the thing feel any lighter, but did temporarily reallocate the pressure. The landscape was peaceful, mostly flat fields of young crops, for this area is almost entirely given to arable farming, and scenically not very exciting. The first high point of my journey came just a few yards past a tiny place named la Cavaterie, where I walked off the right-hand edge of the first of my six maps, and folded it up with a jubilant grunt, prodding it into a side pocket of the backpack. I did a mental celebratory jig, being quite unable to do anything physical apart from remaining upright and keep putting one foot gingerly in front of the other.

At mid-day I plopped down on a patch of grass beneath a feeble sun, and was munching a lump of cheese when a battered van drew up across the road, and three unshaven and unsavoury men sat watching me in a way I didn't much like. Since the lady in St Félix I hadn't seen another human being, and at this moment I felt distinctly alone. So I pulled the sharp stabbing knife from the pocket of my jeans, and staring at the trio with what I hoped was a flinty expression, carved chunks of cheese and ate them from the knife-tip. They sat and watched as I wiped the blade slowly down my jeans, and stabbed it to the hilt in the ground beside me, still staring at them flintily. One said something, and they started the engine and drove away. Whew.

France had not yet awoken from her long winter hibernation, and there was almost no sign of life in the villages but for a few cats and dogs and chickens, and a reedy pond teeming with bellowing frogs. Most restaurants and bars were closed, and many were permanently closed down. I seemed to be the only person about, and the countryside had an oppressive air of desolation. The miles passed painfully but steadily and nothing occurred to break the quiet monotony, except when I came upon two blackbirds fighting savagely. They tumbled to the ground and lay in the road, locked in combat, screeching, pecking, and raking at each other with their claws. It took a fairly substantial prod with the hiking stick to break them apart.

From the west, you enter Dampierre sur Boutonne across a small bridge over the river Boutonne, from where a tall Frenchman and two ladies were admiring the remnants of the tiny, exquisite Renaissance castle that nestles in the elbow of the river on a miniature island.

"Are you going to Compostela?" asked the man, referring to the great pilgrim route which leads to north-west Spain and the town of Compostela, which legend claims to be the burial place of St James the Apostle, whose body is said to have arrived there in a boat bedecked with cockleshells. The cockleshell is the symbol of this pilgrim route, and can be seen etched into many buildings all over France that were and still are staging-posts for the pilgrims

"No, to Geneva."

"Ah yes, you must be English!" he roared. We all laughed at the crazy English.

They asked what route I was taking. I replied that it would be as near as possible to a straight line drawn between La Rochelle and Geneva, apart from a detour to visit some spectacular gorges in central France, but that as I was working my way from campsite to campsite, not wanting to camp alone in the wilds, the line was about as straight as a row of knitting.

One of the ladies walked round behind me, and patted the backpack.

"You look as if you are carrying too much weight. How much does this weigh?"

"Thirty-three pounds."

"NO! That's far too much. We do a lot of walking ourselves. The maximum anyone can carry is twenty-five pounds," said the man. The ladies nodded in agreement, and one of them added: "If you don't reduce the weight, you'll never finish your journey."

I knew they were right, and promised to unload anything that wasn't vital.

Encouraged by their enthusiastic good wishes, and smiling at their exclamation of "You English!" I continued to the campsite. There was no-one else there. As I searched for somewhere to pitch the tent, a smiling man wearing the typical blue overalls of a French workman appeared and beckoned me, indicating a neat mown area bordered by a trim hedge.

"Here," he smiled. "The grass is cut and you will be sheltered by the hedges and the wall."

It was a perfect spot, beside the river, with a backdrop of a small stone bridge and copse of trees.

"You're very lucky. Last week the whole site was twelve inches under water."

It was still pretty soggy.

The village restaurant was closed down, and for sale, so I bought half a dozen eggs, a French stick, and a bottle of cider from the tiny, dusty grocery. I dined on two boiled eggs and a handful of dried apricots, all washed down with the excellent cider, and cooked the remaining eggs into an omelette, which I jammed into the bread for the following day's lunch.

My phone call to Jennifer elicited the information that the weather at home was as cold and miserable as it was here, getting colder and wetter by the hour, and that the geese had chased her all over the place. As she couldn't get outside into the garden, she'd entertained herself dismantling and servicing the stove, after which she'd done the only sensible thing on a day like this, and settled down with a glass of champagne to read and listen to music. She sounded quite cheerful.

After a shower that was a few degrees below tepid, I climbed into the tissue-thin sleeping bag. A woodpecker rapped somewhere close by, and the pigeons gurgled a throaty chorus to a blackbird's song. It was very peaceful, and bitterly cold. I didn't feel Dampierre sur Boutonne had anything to fear from global warming.

There Are Châteaux And Châteaux, And Donkeys And Donkeys

Awakening, (an inexactitude, as through the night I had shivered and rolled around trying not to freeze) to a hard frost and renewed aching back and shoulders, I came to a decision, which was that Nicholas Crane would have to go. The only luxury I carried was his book, *Still Waters Rising*, the inspirational story of his six thousand miles tramp across Europe from Cape Finisterre to Istanbul. His smiling, bespectacled face peered good-naturedly from beneath the silly hat on the book's cover, and I felt a pang as I poked the end of his nose with my finger. He was a great guy, amusing, inspirational, and he had given me a lot of pleasure, but he just had to go. The small and peaceful village was probably as good a place as any for us to part, so together with two pairs of socks, one pair of shorts and a T-shirt all smelling of beer, a large tube of Deep Heat, a roll-on deodorant and the first map which I had finished with, I jammed him into a carrier bag and consigned him to the care of the smiling gardienne, promising to retrieve him in about eight week's time. He would understand.

Being something of a walker himself, he knew that surplus weight simply wouldn't do.

Having dumped Nick, I set off to visit the little Château de Dampierre. There are châteaux and châteaux. Dampierre does not rank as one of the "great" châteaux, whose vulgar opulence was such a poke in the eye to the poor that little wonder they ended up chopping off rich heads. It is simply gorgeous, set upon a tiny island in a bend on the river Boutonne. Designed as both a stronghold and a home it stands on three levels, the lower two bounded by a series of five arches. Originally built at the beginning of the 16th century in the Renaissance style just introduced to France from Italy, but still maintaining a little of the medieval, it served as a replacement and relocation for the original fortified castle that protected Dampierre. During its brief heyday it was an intellectual centre, and a haunt of alchemists, as the many engravings in the stonework testify. The name Dampierre comes from Notre-Dame la Pierre Philosophale— Our Lady of the Philosopher's Stone. During the wars of religion and the French Revolution the little château was sacked and ruined, and it really is difficult to imagine anybody being able to wantonly damage quite such a pretty place. Since 1851 it has been privately owned and restored, and I very much wanted to see inside it. However, it was closed, so with that idea knocked on the head, I started on my way to the next stop, Brioux sur Boutonne.

It took an hour of pallid sunshine before the frost and ice had thawed and the tent had dried. I set off as briskly as the blisters would allow, hoping that the temperature would not slide below zero again during my expedition, because I had just noticed on the thin, light sleeping bag a label indicating that it was only suitable for use in temperatures of 50-80° Fahrenheit.

Despite having abandoned Nick and the other bits and pieces, the backpack didn't feel any lighter, in fact if anything it felt even heavier than before. That was the case for the entire journey— however much I emptied, the weight never became noticeably lighter. It was extraordinary that a handful of items individually weighing nothing could unite to form such a disproportionately heavy load. Never at any time in history could so few little things have weighed so much.

Just outside of Dampierre, there was a sign to *La Maison du Baudet du Poitou* (The House of the Poitou Donkey). This was far too good an opportunity to miss, and worth how ever many extra miles it would add to the day's hike. A tour here would compensate for missing out on the château.

There are donkeys and donkeys, and the *baudet* is really something else. Their primary purpose was originally to cross the stallions with mares of the huge Mulassière breed of horses, in order to produce the prized Poitevin mules. As mechanisation displaced the need for these animals, the *baudet* race declined until, at the start of the 1980s, it was virtually extinct. Then a stud was set up to regenerate the race at La Tillauderie, and it was to here that my path had so fortuitously led.

It was a good two miles diversion to the stud, in, for the first time, warm sunshine. I was the only visitor so early in the day, and able to roam at leisure amongst the docile and friendly Rastafarian equines. They reach up to sixty inches at the shoulder, with fifteen-inch ears, and as adults their coats grow into extremely long, shaggy rusty-brown dreadlocks that are their most distinguishing feature. The lengthy coat, matted with straw and dust, characterises the breed and is not groomed. At La Tillauderie, together with mules and the huge Mulassière horses, the magnificent baudet population is being rebuilt. These kindly giants of the donkey world produce teddy bear foals with dark chocolate, silky soft poodle-hair who jostle gently for attention, together with equally friendly mules and the Mulassière mares and foals. I spent an enchanted hour with these creatures. The centre also houses a fascinating museum showing the history and development of the race, there is a theatre where a video is shown, and guided tours of the stables to meet the stallions and newborn foals.

For the first time since leaving La Rochelle, I wasn't cold. The sun was blazing down. Rather than backtrack to the road, I opted for the forest route to Brioux sur Boutonne. The lady who directed me, and whom I am certain had never carried a backpack weighing about thirty pounds, nor walked miles on feet that were held together with blisters, was determined I should enjoy the most scenic path, despite the fact that it would add nearly six miles to my journey. I really didn't care how beautiful the long route was; in fact I would have traversed a barren wilderness or a disused coalmine, as long as it led to my destination by the shortest possible means. Withered by her scornful shrug, and armed with alarmingly complex directions that I felt were deliberately designed to confuse, I trudged around the woods following a network of narrow strips of dirt, tracks and ruts, trying to guess which was a path and which was not, and seeking with total lack of success the various features which I had been assured would be very apparent.

Eventually, after a very long and hot safari, which led out of the Charente Maritime and into the *département* of Deux Sèvres, I arrived in a village which should have been just one and a half miles from Brioux. Everything about the surroundings corresponded with the map, apart from the cemetery which although very clearly marked on the map, wasn't there in the village. The name on the village notice board was not the same as the name on the map. There were three merry ladies chatting like budgies nearby, and they waved me cheerily into their collective bosom.

"I *am* in le Pontioux, aren't I?" I asked, hoping that if I said it positively enough, it would be so.

"No, but it's not far away," said one of the ladies helpfully. "This is Arsanges."

It certainly seemed well named.

"Le Pontioux is just three and a half miles in that direction."

She pointed northwards. That meant nearly five miles to Brioux. Another two hours agonising walk.

"Come on, we'll put you on the right path."

The cartel danced merrily beside me for a hundred yards seemingly unaware that I was in discomfort as I shuffled and hobbled along and thought dark thoughts. Or maybe they thought I was a poor cripple. I just about was.

"There you are, turn right at the end and just follow the road. *Bon courage.*"

Well, three and a half miles may be no distance by car, bike or horse, or to someone who hasn't already walked over seventeen but to me, then, it sounded unattainably far.

Based on the principle that a positive mental attitude can achieve anything, I kept telling myself that my feet were getting better, but it was a pointless exercise. They were fraying more and more with every step I took. After half an hour of limping along the side of the road, I crumpled in a tearful heap next to a ditch and tugged off the backpack. I simply could not walk any further.

On the other hand, if I didn't, I would have to adjust to the idea of living here beside the road, because the chances of anybody stopping for a heavily laden character wielding a five-foot-long pole that looked like a martial arts weapon were non-existent. This wasn't the spirit that had built an empire, and it wasn't going to get me to a hot shower and somewhere to take off my boots, so the only thing to do was to put my chin up, adopt a stiff upper lip, bite the bullet, and put my best foot forward, et cetera, et cetera, et cetera. But I didn't have a best foot. So I sang instead. *It's a Long Way to Tipperary. The White Cliffs of Dover. Land of Hope and Glory. Two Little Boys. Tie Me Kangaroo Down, Jerusalem* (and did those feeeet). *Tulips from Amsterdam. One Man Went to Mow. The Happy Wanderer. Until I got to Brioux* I was not going to stop singing. If you had ever heard me sing, you would understand how motivated I was to reach it at the earliest possible moment. I was almost jogging by the time I covered the last of the twenty-two miles I'd walked since setting off that morning, and arrived at the deserted campsite. The pleasure of dropping the backpack and shedding the boots was secondary to the joy of not having to listen to the horrible dirge.

A mixture of self-pity and triumph persuaded me that I was due for a reward, so I aimed at a pretty, rustic restaurant offering an excellent menu at an affordable price. Dressed in my cleanest dirty clothes, I enjoyed the luxury of a hot meal and good bottle of wine. Only one other table was occupied, by a party of three —a man and woman who were obviously not married, and the woman's young daughter who was about ten years old. As the adults skirmished playfully, she alternately flirting and freezing, while he plied her attentively with wine and meaningful looks, the child roamed around the room forgotten, looking at paintings, arrangements of flowers, me. I smiled at her and beckoned her over, but she responded by scowling suspiciously and returning to her table where she concentrated on pleating the cloth into a thousand wrinkles.

The restaurant owner's wife came over to chat, and when she heard I was camping, asked whether it wasn't too cold at night. I agreed that it was, and she disappeared, returning a few moments later with a large fluffy blue blanket.

"You can bring it back when you leave," she said.

I rang Jennifer to see how she was managing, and smiled as she recounted some of her experiences so far

"Do you know," she said, "I've been noticing the old men around here are always hiding in the bushes. When I take the horses out and bring them back, I've seen them and acted like I didn't see them. Today I started waving to them. They smile and wave back and go on about their business.

"When I went to the store today I went to ask if Gloria needed anything. She invited me to sit in the garden and have coffee. Susie, this woman's garden is like the garden from hell. Have you seen all that junk her husband's left there? Old cars, rocks, construction equipment? The grass was so high you had to look to see the two Great Danes."

I laughed. "Anything else happened while I've been away?"

"Yeah. When I got home from the store, one of the dogs had jumped the fence around the pond, and gone for a swim. He was soaking wet and trapped inside the fence. He just stood there looking at me like WHO ME?"

I said I was pretty tired and didn't know if I'd walk tomorrow or stay where I was and rest. I'd been lost several times and walked farther than I'd planned, and although I should have been back home on the following day, I didn't think I'd get there for another couple of days.

"Well, you just take things easy and go at your own pace. Everything's just fine here."

The campsite, on the outskirts of the town, also served as the local recreation ground; dog-walkers strolled around the paths and along the riverbank, groups of young children raced around noisily on bicycles and skateboards, while the teenagers sat smoking and talking, hunched earnestly in the cool dusk.

I rolled myself up into the blue blanket, like Cleopatra in the rug, and squirmed into the sleeping bag. From this comforting nest I listened to the children's noise until it faded with the last light, to be replaced by a puppy's anguished squealing and the sinister baying of dogs from a nearby garden, which lasted for hours.

Extract from '*Best Foot Forward - A 500 Mile Walk Through Hidden France*' by Susie Kelly

For links to Amazon Kindle USA, Amazon Kindle UK & Paperback sales pages please go to
http://blackbird-digitalbooks.com

and click on the book cover.

3
I WISH I COULD SAY I WAS SORRY...

With uncompromising honesty and hints of her usual humour, the author describes emigrating, from post-war London in every shade of grey to the technicolour splendour of Kenya, as part of a dysfunctional family. From profound lows to sublime highs, the one constant is her pony, Cinderella. You may shed a tear at her losses, and you will almost certainly be shocked and appalled by what she does for the love of Cinderella.

Prologue

Not long ago I was browsing around Emmaüs in Poitiers. For anybody who doesn't know about the Emmaüs movement, it's a charity that was started by a French hero, Henri Marie Joseph Grouès, more commonly known as Abbé Pierre, who fought ferociously for the rights of the poor and underprivileged. People donate all kinds of things to the movement, from clothes and furnishings to vehicles and valuables. Nothing is wasted. Even nails and screws are carefully collected, sorted and put where they can be found. The shops are a treasure trove for anybody looking for discontinued parts for ancient machines, or collectors and dealers seeking items to sell on for profit.

It's like a giant jumble sale. For a few cents you can buy interesting, pretty items, and in buying them help individuals and families in need. I go there for crockery and glassware because I like unusual things and unmatched table settings.

On my last visit I wandered down to the far end where they sell valuable items that are kept locked up in glass cases. It was the first time I'd ever looked at that part. Next to that are shelves with large ornaments on them, and as I ran my eyes over them, I noticed a collection of clocks. Anniversary clocks. My heart lurched, the room seemed to swim, and I had to get out of there. I put down the plates I had intended to buy and rushed down the stairs, outside into the rain.

Hanworth

Can a child be born strange? Or does it come from some early forgotten experience? My parents and my maternal grandmother, Nan, were loving and caring; we ate well (especially considering that this was just after the end of WWII and many foods were still rationed). Our grey house was comfortable and warm, I had plenty of toys and rag books that Mummy and Nan read to me. I don't think I lacked for anything. So why would I steal?

At the age of five I was a thief. I had a mania for stealing paper. When I could get to school before anybody else, I went around the classroom lifting the lids of the other children's desks and digging into their exercise books with their lined and squared pages. Then, holding my breath with concentration and

70

excitement, quickly, carefully, I would pull out several pages from the centre of each book, bending back any give-away staples that had worked loose. A new day had made a most satisfying start. Why, or what I did with the reams of paper I must have accumulated, I haven't the faintest idea. In our class only my exercise books glowed with plump good health, while my classmates' books were gaunt and skeletal, but the strange thing was that nobody ever seemed to notice. Nothing was mentioned, neither by the victims, nor by the teachers. Each day's anticipation of being named and shamed meant that I was very frightened, but at the same time strangely excited.

Encouraged by my success I began to supplement my paper reserve with money, which had a more practical benefit. Most of the other children in my class brought a 1d. (one penny piece) to school for break-time (this was the 1950s, when there were 12 pennies in a shilling). One penny might not sound much today, but it was sufficient then to buy a fine break-time treat - a choice of a pink or white sugar mouse with a little string tail, Ovaltine or Horlicks tablets folded into a small cone made from paper from used arithmetic exercise books, a packet of lemonade powder eaten from a licked finger, or a small thin chocolate bar. I don't know whether I didn't have my own penny because my parents didn't know about it, or couldn't afford it. In any event it didn't matter because as we stood beside our desks for morning prayers, our hands devoutly folded and eyes piously squeezed shut, I reached out and felt for the penny pieces nearest to me, put on the corner of their desks by their unsuspecting owners. With a nimble movement my hand found the coins and transferred them into the pocket of my gymslip. On a bumper day I managed to scoop two coins, careful not to let them clink together as they changed ownership. Astonishingly, none of my classmates ever mentioned the loss of their pennies, just as they didn't appear to notice that their exercise books were showing signs of anorexia. If I'd had a penny to lose you can be pretty sure I would have raised quite a storm if it had disappeared. So each day some unfortunate child, or on a good day, two children, didn't get a sugar mouse or similar treat. The Lord helps those who help themselves, and he certainly provided very nicely for me.

Apart from paper and pennies I began to find small, interesting items in other children's desks. Like a jackdaw I pecked them up. My satchel was a repository of things that did not belong to me – hair grips, pencils, tiny ornaments. It was the mother-of-pearl rosary beads and Bible that led to my downfall. On an early-morning raid, I was enthralled to find these pretty items in another child's desk. I slipped them into my satchel, so thrilled with this exceptional haul that I didn't even bother about harvesting any paper.

That evening there was a knock at our front door, a rare event, and my mother came and said there was someone to see me. It was the previous owner of my swag, with her parents.

It's only now, as I write this, that I think: How had they known where to come? How had they known it was me? It's most unlikely that they would have gone to the house of each child in the class. They wouldn't have had a car, in those days almost nobody did, so they would have either had to walk or travel by bus. I'm sure, now, that they had somehow known who the thief was and come straight to our house. Is it possible that my clandestine stealing sessions were observed, not as secret as I thought? Was I watched as I pilfered? Did the watcher know about the pennies and the paper?

"Susan," asked my mother, "did you bring home some things belonging to Angela?" The dispossessed little girl gazed at me, wide-eyed and open-mouthed.

"Yes," I said. I was a thief, not a liar.

"Then will you go and get them, and give them back like a good girl?"

Off I trotted and with a slight reluctance returned the pretty things to their owner. Then everybody made a great fuss of me. Angela's mother invited me to tea at their house, where she gave me a packet of waxed crayons and a new Bible. I never wanted to steal anything again.

Post-war London, where I was born, was a landscape in every shade of grey. Our semi-detached house was grey, in a grey road in a grey place called Hanworth in the now administratively-defunct county of Middlesex, south-west London.

At that time, we were a respectable middle-class family, like hundreds of thousands of similar families. My mild and gentle father worked for Kodak, and Mummy was a housewife and mother. We were the only family in the street who owned a motor vehicle – a motorcycle and sidecar my father used for travelling to and from work, and for pleasure rides. Mummy rode on the pillion with her arms around my father and I sat in the little pod with its slightly hazy plastic windows. We had a black cat called Clem, named after Clement Attlee, the British Prime Minister. Clem's favourite spot was curled up asleep in my father's old leather attaché case in the garden.

On Sunday mornings my father liked to walk, and if I went with him I had to jog smartly to keep up with his long stride. Those walks took us to nearby Teddington Lock on the river Thames, and Royal Bushy Park where we played cricket, my father bowling slow balls and me trying to whack them back with a child's cricket bat. The highlight of our visits to the park was a ride on Bonny Bright Eyes, the playground rocking horse that seated several passengers.

At weekends, Mummy's mother, Nan, came to visit with her corgi, Taffy. During the war she, like so many others had "dug for victory" and it was something she had enjoyed and continued. She spent Saturdays weeding, hoeing, sowing, planting, staking and harvesting boxes of beautiful vegetables and fruit. Short, dignified and plump, she was beautifully spoken and always impeccably dressed. Her passion was music. Both her paternal grandparents were opera singers; her father was a chorister at Westminster Abbey and her uncle a chorister at St Paul's Cathedral. She had trained to be an opera singer and sung in the chorus of many operas with the great names of the time. Later, when her voice began to let her down she became a secretary, and worked for one of the senior directors of the General Electric Company. During the First World War she had married an American serviceman and emigrated to the United States. It was an unhappy marriage and after two years she returned to England with her little daughter – my mother. Although she never mentioned it, the stigma and difficulties of being a divorcée and single mother in the 1920s must have been considerable.

She was the quintessentially doting grandmother who would do and give me anything I asked for. For a while I had an obsession with posting presents to myself. Nan would find small things like her powder compact, a tiny scent bottle or a writing pad, and together we carefully wrapped them in brown paper, tied them with string and addressed to me. Then we walked hand-in-hand to the Post Office to buy stamps and drop the packet into the letter box. When it was delivered the following day I was beside myself with excitement. A week or so later it was recycled and re-posted, and no matter how many times I sent myself the same thing, the delight of receiving it never diminished.

Our next door neighbour was a tall, thin man with a long black beard, always dressed in black and always wearing a large black hat. Whenever our paths crossed he smiled and said "Hello". My father hurried me past, telling me not to speak to him because he was a Jew. I asked once what a Jew was as he looked much like any other person, but my father simply said they weren't like us. I tried pressing the question, in what way weren't they like us, but there didn't seem to be a proper explanation. I spent the next twenty years wondering exactly what it was about Jews that made them "not like us." It's strange that such a quiet and easy-going man as my father should have been a bigot. He also hated Germans which was more understandable, as he'd served in the British army for the duration of WWII and his uncle had been killed at Dunkirk.

Directly opposite our house lived Mummy's friend Auntie Kitty. Tall and thin with a chuckly voice, wiry black hair and a prominent wart on her chin, Auntie Kitty became a celebrity in our street when she bought a television in 1953 so that she and we could watch the Coronation. I recall that the sound was very clear – the harsh, unfaltering voice of our new Queen as she made her first public address, although the black and white picture flickered on and off and the small screen seemed to be enveloped in a snow storm. It was a freezing day and a long afternoon, punctuated by servings of Auntie Kitty's speciality. Soaked in a mixture of egg and milk, cooked in lard and saturated with sugar, her fried jam sandwiches were ambrosial. When Auntie Kitty's big chin wart began sprouting hairs, Mummy persuaded her to do something about it, and so we went by bus with her one day to hospital to have it removed. All the way home we laughed at her delight in not having the thing on her chin any more. Wherever Mummy was, there was always laughter.

Once a year we went on holiday with Nan to Boscombe, east of Bournemouth on England's south coast. After breakfast at the guesthouse on the Lansdowne Road, we marched down the long zigzag path to the sandy beach with its fascinating pools of slimy, podded weed and furtive creatures scuttling and darting beneath rocks. My ruched red swimming costume held water, so as I emerged from the sea it drooped around my knees as the water drained away.

Looking back, I recall the weather was always perfect, never a cloud or drop of rain to spoil the blue of the sky and the kiss of the sun. Boscombe meant being with my parents and Nan all day, every day, ice cream, pony rides, mini-golf, building sandcastles and then watching the incoming tide melt them away. At the end of the day the haul back up the long zigzag path was hard work for small, tired legs.

Those memories of the early years of my life are of security and love. As my father was at work I saw less of him than Mummy, and he was not as demonstrative as her, but I adored him.

I have pin clear mental photos of our life in Hanworth.

On the kitchen table sit rows of fragrant small sponge cakes in fluted wax paper cases. When they are cool, Mummy slices off the tops and cuts them in half. She spreads butter cream over the base and sticks the two pieces on top, like wings. She calls them "Butterfly cakes," and always leaves a generous amount of delicious raw cake mixture in the mixing bowl for me to eat with a wooden spoon. Even today when I make a cake and take a spoonful of the raw mixture and close my eyes, I see and smell the butterfly cakes on our kitchen table.

While I sit on the draining board with my feet in the kitchen sink, Mummy works her way down from my face to my feet with a flannel dipped in the warm, soapy water. When she washes my hair she gives me a flannel to press against my eyes to stop the shampoo stinging them. We run our fingers through my wet hair. If it squeaks then we know it's clean. Then she wraps me in a towel and pats me dry, feeds me into my pyjamas and warm blue dressing gown with the ladybird buttons.

The dressing gown has a cord of twisted blue and silver, with tassels on the end. Alone in the living room in front of the coal fire covered by a wire safety guard, I swing the dressing gown's tasselled cord into the flames so that it singes with a satisfying sizzly noise and an interesting smell. Mummy sniffs when she comes into the room, and looks in puzzlement at the carpet in front of the fire for signs of smouldering.

The fire can be a bit of a sod to start. My father holds sheets of newspaper across the sullen chimney to encourage the draught. Putrid smoke billows, then a small flame grows, singeing the paper yellow. Half an hour later the coals glow orange as we sit listening to the radio. Clem gets as close as he can to the fire. Mummy knits or smocks clothes for me and my father puffs on his pipe.

All our walls are painted the same dull cream colour, so my father decorates the living room with a bucket of distemper. It's a thick green stuff the colour of baby's diarrhoea, and he blobs it onto the wall with a roller. It looks horrible.

At weekends Nan is in the garden with Taffy, rain or shine, always planting or picking. I don't remember Mummy doing anything in the garden apart from rescuing birds from Clem. She stows them tenderly into a cardboard shoe box and puts them in the airing cupboard to recover. Usually they regain their senses and equilibrium after a couple of hours, and fly away to safety. Or straight back into Clem. Daddy doesn't garden, either, but he likes pansies because they have happy little faces.

Nan eats Energen Rolls because she is trying to lose weight. They are crispy on the outside and crispy within, but not very satisfying. I prefer Taffy's charcoal dog biscuits.

Once we go to visit Daddy's parents. There is a long, gloomy, dark green corridor and two and a half flights of stairs. At the top is a bedroom where a skeletal yellow-skinned woman lies in bed coughing.

Mummy comes home from the Ideal Homes Exhibition, merry, footsore and laden with carrier bags stuffed with miniature pots of jam.

She takes me to Bentalls in Kingston to have my hair cut, and then we have tea and toasted teacakes oozing with butter. We bring home one of their cakes shaped like a giant mushroom and made from marzipan and lashings of coffee cream.

Every Friday evening she coos with delight over a box of powdery Turkish delight, Payne's Poppets or Buttered Brazil Nuts, her weekly treat from Daddy.

She is always happy, smiling and beautiful, with short curly dark hair, golden hazel eyes and a carefully-pencilled black beauty spot to the side of her mouth.

In the summer she ties ribbons in my silver blonde hair, and sews pretty smocked dresses. During the winter months I wear a pair of rust-coloured Harris tweed leggings, and a liberty bodice beneath a knitted jumper. The leggings are thick hairy trousers with a broad elastic band that passes underneath my shoes to hold the trousers down over my ankles. Wearing them can best be likened to having both legs scrubbed with medium grade steel wool: they have an abrasive quality that makes each step torture. Mummy takes great pride in dressing me in style, and these horrid trousers must be the dernier cri. She can't have the least idea of what torment it is to wear them. The liberty bodice is a less painful, more private garment, a short, white fleecy sleeveless thing with rubber buttons and little rubbery suspenders to hold up the thick brown wrinkly stockings that we wear to school; it fits under a chunky woolly vest that lies beneath various other layers of clothing culminating in a hand-knitted jumper all designed to keep the penetrating damp of English winters at bay. My hair is tucked beneath a bright red knitted pixie bonnet, tight-fitting like a snood and reaching to a nipple on the crown of my head. The rust-coloured leggings and the red pixie hat add quite a splash of colour to the generally grey environment.

On my sideboard today is a sepia photograph of a handsome blonde five-year-old boy. He's wearing a one-piece woollen bathing costume with straps over the shoulders, sitting on a rock on a beach, smiling into the sun. This is my brother Ian, born in October of 1940, the height of the Blitz on London.

I suppose it was because Mummy would have been working during the war that he was sent to live with an elderly couple in Devon. All I know is that in February 1945, Ian's temporary foster parents wrote to tell Mummy that he was ill, with a seemingly permanent cold. She went to Devon, where the doctor told her that Ian had meningitis. There was no treatment, no cure and no hope. It was only a matter of time. He died with Mummy sitting by his bed and his father in North Africa. I cannot begin to imagine how they were affected by this loss, how my father felt when he learned the news, so far away, and how my mother coped with the loss of her child as well as the absence of and worry about her husband.

Probably it was for this sad reason that my birthday and Christmas presents were always things like a bus conductor's costume, complete with a punching machine and tickets, or a Meccano set in the form of a crane with a little handle to wind it up and down to pick up matchboxes. My father made small contraptions from a cotton reel, a rubber band and a length of candle. When the rubber band had been twisted sufficiently the cotton reel jerked across the floor in a purposeful way like a little tank. I was never given the things I really wanted, and asked for repeatedly: a glass eye, a hearing aid, and a set of false teeth. I still don't have any of them.

Each year, Kodak held a party at their offices in Kingsway, London for the children of their staff. Whether all the children found it as much of an ordeal as I did, I don't know. But none of us knew each other and I seem to remember that I couldn't wait to go home, with my slice of cake, balloon and gift-wrapped present.

There were only two things that darkened my days and nights. The monster that lived upstairs in the toilet bowl, skulking with evil intentions until the toilet was flushed, when it would spring out and rake at people's bottoms with hooked claws and spiky teeth. From terror of these awful assaults I developed a technique of opening the door wide, reaching in and yanking on the chain and leaping down the adjacent staircase before the monster could get me, crashing to the bottom of the stairs with my knickers around my ankles and alarming Mummy.

And there was Mr Beeblesticks, who lived in the big wardrobe in my bedroom (where I hid from Mummy and the knife – I'll come to that later). Mr Beeblesticks was a friend by day, but at night, once the bedroom light was turned out he became a gun-wielding murderer. So that his bullets would miss, I lay in my bed rocking madly from side to side. The rocking habit lasted until I got married, I just couldn't get to sleep unless I kept madly rolling backwards and forwards.

I didn't mention either of these horrors to my parents, because I didn't want to worry them.

Where did these strange ideas originate, these evil people who wanted to kill me? I was safe, secure and very well loved. The Saturday morning matinees at the cinema showed only cartoons, and the most violent programs I watched on Auntie Kitty's television were Bill and Ben the Flowerpot Men, Andy Pandy, Noddy and Muffin the Mule.

Even stranger was the recurring nightmare I had for years. I was alone on an empty, sandy beach on a hot sunny day, with cliffs rising close behind me. As I watched the surf swishing gently backwards and forwards, the sea suddenly began to withdraw to the far horizon, leaving just the clean sand behind. Soon there was no sea at all, just the pristine beach. In the far distance a darkness appeared on the skyline. It began moving towards where I was standing. As it neared, it developed into a great wave, curling upwards. It rushed quickly forwards. It grew until it was the height of the cliffs behind, and I was beneath it, looking up, knowing that now the water would come crashing down and wash me away.

I'd certainly never heard of or seen a tsunami, so where did this image come from? Was it an omen, a warning of what was to come?

But these were only small blips in a very happy and normal family life filled with love and laughs and cuddles and hugs.

The convent school where I went to appropriate anything light enough to lift, not nailed down and small enough to fit in my satchel was in Sunbury-on-Thames, two bus-rides from Hanworth. Mummy walked me to the nearest bus stop, a couple of hundred yards from our house and put me on the first bus. This bus stopped at Sunbury-on-Thames where I changed to a second bus, which stopped a short distance from the school. From the bus stop I crossed a major road, although at that time there was little traffic, and then walked up a long winding rhododendron-lined drive. It's unthinkable to imagine five-year-old children undertaking such a journey alone these days, but at that time it was perfectly normal. One small girl in our class caught a train unaccompanied to and from school. At her invitation I went home with her one day, to the considerable consternation of her mother who had no idea she was expecting a guest. She had to take me back by train and bus to where my mother was panicking at my failure to arrive home.

In the classroom, before reading or writing, or sums or drawing we learned the Ten Commandments. We learned them by heart, by constant chanted repetition: Thou shalt not this, thou shalt not that. You mustn't do idolatry or adultery and you mustn't steal (I think that was No. 7). If you did any of these things then you could not go to Heaven. Instead you would burn in Purgatory and have to suffer very much indeed forever and ever; but even this fearsome prospect did not deter or frighten me from stealing paper and money, despite the great black sin blotches I knew were printed all over my wicked little soul, which would be a dead giveaway on the Day of Judgement.

We were not a religious family. I think we called ourselves Church of England, but as far as I remember the family only went to church to deliver me to Sunday school. Like my weekly dancing and elocution lessons, a convent education would, my parents believed, make me into a little lady.

The only time I ever remember Mummy being angry was when I was eating. I was a slow eater and had difficulty swallowing. It wasn't that I was fussy. I'd eat anything except angelica, with which Mummy decorated the trifle, but I could chew soup or ice cream for hours on end, churning it around and around in my mouth like cement swishing in a mixer, until Mummy screamed: "For God's sake, *swallow* it!" But the harder I tried, the less I could swallow, so I chewed and swished faster and faster. One day when I was struggling with a mouthful of tomato soup, she picked up a knife and frightened me so much I ran upstairs and shut myself in the wardrobe where Mr Beeblesticks lived.

When I ventured out, Mummy was sitting sobbing on my bed, and I don't know which of us was the more traumatised.

After that I ate my meals with our friends the Mason family who lived on the opposite side of the fence at the bottom of our garden. Daddy removed a plank from the fence so that I didn't have to go around by the road. The Masons had a little boy called Charles, who was quite happy for me to sit churning in their dining room while he watched and waited patiently for the final gulp that released us to play. He must have been quite a precocious little boy, because the game we played most was "r" for rudies, which mainly consisted of watching each other urinate into a small bowl in his bedroom. I think I probably got more out of this than he did. The casual way he asked in front of his parents if I wanted to go and play "r" used to make me hot and crimson with embarrassment. I was certain that his mother and father were perfectly aware of our urinary adventures.

One morning, left to our own devices, Charles and I raided my house of anything small enough to lift, and set it all outside to sell. In those days there was almost no motor traffic about. Milk and coal were still delivered by horse-drawn carts, policemen patrolled on foot and people went to work by public transport, so we could safely spread out our wares across the street without worrying. Whose idea this had been or why, I'm not sure, but possibly we'd run out of urine. Nan arrived just in time to save

Mummy's twelve treasured Apostle spoons going off with a stranger for one penny.

Kenya Castle

In 1954, I turned eight. In the diarrhoea-coloured front room a dozen of my school friends were enjoying jam tarts, butterfly cakes, lemon curd sandwiches with the crusts removed, jelly in waxed paper bowls and a pink blancmange rabbit. We were having a party to celebrate not only my birthday, but also some very exciting news. Mummy clapped her hands, and two rows of little faces gawped at her as she put a finger to her lips, signalling silence. Soon, she said, our family would be leaving England and going to live in Africa. We all clapped enthusiastically and shouted "Hurray!" It was a shame that my friends wouldn't be coming with us, but on the other hand it was going to be a great adventure. Based on a Tarzan film I'd recently seen I expected our new home to be a tree house reached by swinging through the jungle on trailing foliage. I could already see myself waving to passing monkeys and riding around on elephants. I couldn't wait to get there.

In August 1954, we climbed into a taxi and left the grey house in the grey street to spend our last night in England at a hotel in central London. Driving through the streets we passed rows and blocks of buildings crumbling into chunks of brick and clouds of dust. Great iron balls swung from cranes into walls, collapsing them likes castles of cards. As the walls fell away they revealed wallpaper and pictures still hanging in rooms that would never be lived in again. It was like looking at a collection of broken dolls' houses. Nine years after the end of WWII, parts of London were still in a frightful mess.

The hotel was a palace of thick carpets, long corridors, polished banisters, sumptuous rooms and electric lights left on all the time. Sitting in the grand dining room for our evening meals and breakfasts the following morning, I imagined that even our new Queen couldn't be living in greater splendour than we were.

Nan had come to see us off at Tilbury docks. She had already lost a grandson; now she was here to see her only child and granddaughter leaving to live more than 4,000 miles away, in a country in a state of emergency due to the Mau Mau uprising. With our departure she'd have no family left in England. It would be four years before we'd see her again, when my father's first long leave would be due and we'd all come back to England for a holiday. Or that is what we thought.

The gangway trembled as we boarded the S. S. Kenya Castle. Elegant, red-funnelled, lavender-coloured, one of the fleet of the Union Castle Steamship Company, she would take us to our new life. Noise and confusion, seamen scurrying around, luggage being hauled aboard, paper streamers in the air, a feeling of elation tinged with sadness. As the liner pulled away from the docks to the mournful blaring of the ship's horn, Mummy cried. We waved to the tiny figure of Nan standing on the dock far below, one hand raised in a sad farewell, growing ever smaller as the ship pulled away, until she was gone from sight.

In those days air travel was a relatively new and far more expensive method of travel, something reserved for the wealthy. But for us life aboard this opulent floating hotel was indescribably exciting. From the grey street in Hanworth and the routine of everyday life we were transported to a new world. Our cabin was luxurious, with its own bathroom. There was a swimming pool, games rooms, cinemas, libraries, shops and an ever-changing and ever more colourful scenery. The dining tables wore starched white linen cloths, and the menus changed daily. Fourteen years of food rationing in Britain had only ended in July; breakfast at home had been toast and jam or marmalade. Now we could choose from a variety of cereals, stewed and fresh fruits that became increasingly exotic as the ship ploughed southwards; eggs cooked to order, kidneys, kippers, bacon, sausages, kedgeree, toast and butter and a choice of jams. We were spoiled for choice. At mid-morning each day, white-uniformed stewards walked the decks where passengers sat on chairs or loungers with blankets over their knees, serving cups of hot Bovril. As we advanced southwards, Bovril gave way to strawberry and vanilla ice creams in little cartons eaten with wooden spatulas. At home they had been an occasional summer treat, but now were in abundance. There was a daily quota of these ice creams, and any surplus was tossed overboard, to bob and swirl in the foaming wake of the ship. I was sorry I couldn't eat more, but even ice cream took a lot of chewing.

Lunch was another feast, followed by afternoon tea served in the library. Instead of the Sandwich Spread or Shippams fish paste sandwiches that had been our staple tea in Hanworth, there were tiered trays of neat triangular sandwiches, dainty iced cakes and tea poured from silver teapots into china cups.

Children's evening meal was served early, before the adults who were expected to dress formally for dinner. I used to sit in my pyjamas on a balcony, looking down on the dining room where glasses chinked and waiters weaved between the tables with laden trays. My father, tall and very slim with fair hair and a neat matching moustache, and Mummy with her sparkling eyes and wide smile were a striking couple. To me they were indisputably the most glamorous parents on the ship, standing out amongst the crowd, dancing after dinner in each other's arms to the ship's orchestra.

Every day there were organised activities – films, games and fancy dress competitions – I won a prize as a little pink crepe-paper rosebud. Deck games for adults – quoits, clay pigeon shooting, crazy races and the daily sweepstake that involved calculating how far the ship would progress during the next twenty-four hours. Passengers enjoyed constant entertainment from morning to night, day after day. All day, every day. Mummy, Daddy and me together.

The Kenya Castle carved her way down the western coast of France, through the Bay of Biscay and along the Spanish and Portuguese coastline, stopping in Gibraltar where we laughed at the antics of the apes. In the Mediterranean heat, Mummy and I flagged and came up in itchy bumps. From his wartime service in North Africa and Italy, Daddy was less affected, although his fair complexion resembled a boiled prawn. In Port Said and Port Sudan, we sat at rickety tables in dirty places, drinking hot lemonade and batting at clouds of flies and bluebottles that swarmed around our faces, sipped from the spill on the tables and crawled into our sticky glasses.

I'll never forget sailing through the Suez Canal. Silhouettes of camels, donkeys, men and children glided past on the palmy sandbanks as the sun folded itself from a brilliant red ball into a sliver that slid gracefully from sight into the blackness of the night. During the day hordes of noisy Arab children besieged the ship, clambering up rope ladders from little boats, winching up to the decks leather pouffes and whips, camel stools, brassware, all manner of interesting and exciting things, and screaming prices that halved, halved and halved again until a deal was struck. The magic gully-gully man in his long white robe sat cross-legged on the deck and produced from thin air, our pockets or the backs of our necks tiny yellow chicks until the deck was overrun with little balls of yellow fuzz. The heat was stifling, and my nose bled copiously. Where the Suez Canal issued into the Red Sea, we stopped in the unspeakable heat of Aden for cheap duty-free shopping.

The Red Sea bled into the Indian Ocean as we followed the African coastline. Crossing the Equator poor King Neptune, in keeping with tradition had to be dunked into the swimming pool, and I seem to remember that he had a bucket of eggs thrown over him too for our entertainment.

When we hove into Kilindini docks in Mombasa, my first feeling was one of tremendous disappointment. There were tarmac roads, modern buildings, motor vehicles and not a single tree house, jungle or elephant in sight. But the disappointment was fleeting, erased by the noise of cranes unloading cargo, the rattling of unleashed chains, ships' horns moaning, vehicles hooting. Laughing barefoot Africans dressed in only khaki shorts glistened black beneath the sun, heaving loads and pushing top-heavy wobbly wooden carts. The smell was of salt water and spices, hot tar, hot leather luggage and sweat. It was a scene completely alien to anything I could have imagined, and overwhelmingly seductive.

Once our luggage was unloaded and processed in the corrugated iron shed that was the Customs Office, we moved on to the final stage of our safari, the train journey from Mombasa to Nairobi, on what was known as the Lunatic Line. I am really very grateful to Linda Watanabe McFerrin for her permission to quote from the following beautifully evocative description of the Mombasa-Nairobi railway line, which she has put into words far better than I could ever hope to do.

"I sat back on my narrow bunk on the Kenya Railways train that runs nightly from Nairobi to Mombasa, pulled up the window shade and surveyed the exterior landscape. Outside the railcar, the dark continent was truly dark. I saw giraffe, elephants, wildebeest, zebra -- herds of fantastic ebony creatures on the move. But, in truth, they were only baobab trees, kapoks, thorn trees, bush -- denizens of the vegetable kingdom transformed, by starlight and my imagination, into animals. By day, the high plains around Nairobi would, in fact, be grazed by these creatures, but for now -- moving in comforting shadow toward slumber -- this menagerie of fancy seemed most appropriate. I was, after all, aboard the Lunatic Express, a line that, to conventional minds, had always been a bit far-fetched.

"It was an eccentric enterprise and therefore perfectly suited to the British temperament of the late 19th Century. Nevertheless, when the Imperial British East Africa Company proposed its scheme to lay track from the East African coast into the unsettled interior, the critics stood up and raised voices. Media dubbed the proposed railway a "lunatic line." According to the plan, the Central African Railway, starting at Mombasa, would move through 657 miles of African bush past a little-known Masai watering hole, at the time called enkare nyarobe or "sweet water," over the Great Rift Valley, across the equatorial highlands and down to the shores of Lake Victoria where steamships could continue the route through Uganda.

"It would, supporters conjectured, put an end to the slave trade which originated, in part, in Uganda and to which the British were opposed; and it would provide a route via Lake Victoria and the Nile through British East Africa that would link the ports of the Indian Ocean to the Mediterranean Sea. Of course, at the time, there was no one to service along the way, but strategically, it seemed like a very sound move. They could build it at a cost of £ 3,685,400.

"They were energetic. They were optimistic. They were wrong.

"First, they'd have to build a new port to accommodate the supply ships. Termites would devour the wooden risers as fast as they laid them; lions would devour the workers; dysentery, tsetse flies, hostile tribes and malaria would pick off the survivors, and torrential rains would wash away what the

86

termites had missed. It would end up costing almost twice the estimate. It would take nearly a decade to complete. At the end of the first year, they would have progressed a pitiful twenty-four miles inland.

"It was a heroic endeavour, and in spite of the obstacles, it was an insanely brilliant success. It made white settlement of the East African highlands possible. When completed, it shortened the journey from Mombasa to Nairobi from six weeks to twenty-four hours. But the name, "Lunatic Express," stuck and rightly so."

"What it will cost no words can express;
What is its object no brain can suppose;
Where it will start from no one can guess;
Where it is going nobody knows;
What is the use of it none can conjecture;
What it will carry there's none can define;
And in spite of George Curzon's superior lecture,
It clearly is naught but a lunatic line.
London Magazine Truth, 1896"

It was late afternoon when our train pulled out of Mombasa's frenzied railway station. For a short time we could watch the passing landscape of banana trees and coconut palms like vast umbrellas, thatched mud huts and, to my 8-year-old eyes, embarrassingly bare-breasted black ladies. Their naked little pot-bellied children, with teeth startlingly white against their brown skin, sat in the dust, smiling and waving enthusiastically as the train passed.

Night falls abruptly and early in Africa, and soon there was nothing to see except blackness. A steward came and converted our seats into bunk beds, made up with thick, cool white linen sheets and heavy, dark green scratchy blankets. It is a 300-mile journey to Nairobi, uphill all the way from sea level to 5,500 feet and the train struggled along the tracks, at times hardly above walking pace. We ate in the dining car at tables laid with starched white cloths and lit by small table lamps. Our meals were served by soft-voiced black men, barefoot, wearing dazzling white gloves and starched khanzus - ankle-length garments like nightshirts - and black-tasselled red fezzes on their heads. The train jolted gently through the night as it ground its way through the vast wild African countryside.

The next morning we raised the blinds for our first view of the dusty, flat Athi plains, 40 miles south of Nairobi. The brown landscape was dotted with thorn trees and teemed with animals – giraffe, zebras, wildebeest, warthogs, hyenas, Thompson and Grant gazelles, in their hundreds and in their thousands.

As wondrous a sight as this was, I was still concerned because there were still no signs of any tree houses, and not even the shadow of an elephant.

Nairobi

Nairobi railway station was a cauldron of excitement, colour, stenches and commotion. Velvety, rumbling African voices and gentle laughter, urgent shouts, the occasional roar of a donkey; impatient hooting vehicles; ghastly odours of rotting vegetables enhanced by the heat of the sun already high by early morning; gleaming black skin, huge white smiles, eager hands loading luggage onto handcarts. We stood in a small family huddle amidst this new world, and despite my disappointment that it was not a liana-festooned jungle populated by wild animals and tree-houses, I was enchanted by the Technicolor magic of this foreign land.

One of my father's new colleagues arrived at the station to take us to what would be our temporary accommodation until our furniture arrived from England. He drove us to Plums Hotel up what was then known as Princess Elizabeth Highway. The wide multi-carriageway was lined with crimson Nandi flame and blue Jacaranda trees, punctuated by roundabouts ablaze with bougainvillea in all its flamboyant colours – purple, crimson, scarlet, pale orange, Persil white. Everywhere there was colour and open space and blue skies and the caress of the sun.

At the hotel we stayed in a "banda," a self-contained cottage set amongst lush sprinkled lawns. Creamy frangipani blossoms, with their velvety orange hearts perfumed the air. Grey lizards flittered through piles of stones and up the walls, disappearing when I tried to catch them, and leaving behind their wriggling tails as a defiant souvenir. Long-tailed mousebirds bathed in the dust; bright yellow weaver birds built their intricate nest colonies and iridescent glossy starlings ravaged the loquat trees. In the hotel dining room were long menus to choose from, of both familiar and completely strange dishes, particularly the fresh fruit – pineapples, bananas, sticky mangoes, sickly sweet papaya, tangy passion fruit and creamy avocado pears. Until then the most foreign fruit I'd tasted was the tangerine tucked in the toe of my Christmas stocking next to the handful of nuts and small net bag of chocolate coins.

Each night, one of the hotel staff came to the banda with a giant flit gun, and enthusiastically pumped every corner and crevice with a stinking and choking substance designed to kill mosquitoes. It probably did us more harm than them. White mosquito nets hung from the ceiling and had to be tucked in all around the edge of our beds, but there always seemed to be small holes somewhere that allowed the enterprising, resilient mosquitoes to find their way through and bite us, leaving pink itchy lumps. If you gouged a cross in the bites by digging a fingernail really hard into them it stopped the itching, until the pain from the fingernail subsided.

When our furniture arrived we moved into a spacious bungalow on the Lower Kabete Road in the area called Westlands, a residential suburb some five miles from the centre of Nairobi town. Adjacent to the bungalow was a small guesthouse where the then Governor of Kenya, Sir Evelyn Baring's secretary lived. The properties belonged to one of the most charismatic characters ever to leave his footprints on the continent of Africa, Colonel Ewart Grogan, swashbuckling pioneer and legendary hunter. He was outspoken and controversial in his views on the British administration of Kenya, owned half a million acres of land, and was the first man to walk from Cape Town to Cairo, to prove to his future father-in-law that he was of suitable matrimonial fibre.

He would have been in his 80s, a tall, upright gentleman, white-haired and white-bearded – he reminded me of pictures I'd seen of Buffalo Bill - when he arrived unannounced by taxi at our house one day. He had just remembered leaving £10,000 (a phenomenal amount today, let alone then) in notes on top of a wardrobe in one of our bedrooms. As the wardrobes were built-in and reached right to the ceiling, there was no "on top" to them. He was very confused and anxious, and couldn't understand where the wardrobe's top had gone. He insisted on climbing on a chair to feel that it wasn't there for himself. My father drove him to the railway station to put him on a train back to Mombasa, near where he lived. Leaving me standing on the platform, my father helped him aboard, but it took so long to settle the Colonel into his carriage that the train started pulling slowly away, leaving me howling with fright at the sight of my disappearing parent, who daringly leapt from the train just before he ran out of platform.

Apart from being our landlord, the Colonel would have, indirectly, an enormous influence over my life. In memory of the wife he had walked so far to win, he had founded in her name a children's hospital in Nairobi, Gertrude's Garden. In less than a year, I would be lying in that hospital, catalysing the drama that would affect our family for decades.

Extract from *I Wish I Could Say I Was Sorry...* by Susie Kelly c. Susie Kelly 2013

For links to Amazon Kindle USA, Amazon Kindle UK & Paperback sales pages please go to
http://blackbird-digitalbooks.com
 and click on the book cover.

4

THE VALLEY OF HEAVEN AND HELL
Cycling In The Shadow Of Marie Antoinette

Alongside her energetic and resourceful husband (when he's not zooming on ahead), Susie follows the identical route taken by Marie-Antoinette and Louis XVI when they tried to escape from the Revolution, and their journey back to their executions. Her route takes her from Versailles to the vineyards and champagne cellars of Epernay and Reims then through the Marne valley, the scene of unimaginable horror and devastation during World War 1.

"Get a bicycle. You will not regret it if you live." Mark Twain

It is 3.00pm in a small back road in Versailles. I am straddling my bicycle, cold, frightened and growing wetter by the minute, courtesy of a delicate but determined drizzle. Our waterproof clothing is carefully rolled and stowed at the bottom of our luggage, because when we packed our panniers this morning the clear blue skies had given no indication that they would only be of a very temporary nature. We are setting off to cycle first to Paris, and then half-way across France. An undertaking for which I recognise only now, at this very late stage, I am totally unprepared mentally, and unsuited physically. I am angry with myself for agreeing to it in the first place, and even angrier for feeling so feeble about it now. I open my mouth to call out to Terry, a few yards ahead of me, to say I've changed my mind about this venture. Just as I do so he slings his leg effortlessly over his bike, waves his arm above his head and bellows over his shoulder "Forward ho!" I am reminded of John Wayne saddling up and moving out a wagon train. He shoots away like a rocket as I screech at his receding back; but he's already vanished around the corner.

Quickly checking that the baking tray behind my saddle is firmly secured, I hesitantly launch away from the pavement. The bike wobbles and whirrs forward, down to the junction with the main road, which is teeming with traffic. Our three months of training for this expedition have been on quiet country lanes where we count the traffic as heavy if more than four vehicles pass in an hour.

By now a hundred yards ahead, Terry has stopped and is looking back. Taking one hand from the handlebars, and nearly falling off as a result, I raise my arm authoritatively, to signal that he must stay just where he is, not move another inch. Misinterpreting my message, he understands that all is well. Away he pedals again, leaving me muttering dementedly, using alternate cuffs to wipe the rain from my glasses - a futile effort - and cringeing as convoys of coaches pass mere inches from my handlebars; from steamed-up windows rows of pink face-blobs peer out into the murk. I envy them their safety and comfort. The spray from passing vehicles unites with the drizzle to force itself through my clothes right down to my skin. Wheels in the gutter, elbows clenched to my sides, this is my first ever experience of cycling in heavy traffic. I am not enjoying it yet.

Terry is now 500 yards ahead; through the underwater effect of my glasses I can vaguely discern the blurred red shape of the panniers on his bike. Every traffic light in Versailles changes to red as I approach, further widening the distance between us. I'm forced to dismount and make a new wobblesome beginning each time the lights switch to green. I imagine a malevolent little man sitting in a traffic control box, watching my progress and gleefully pushing a button to make things as difficult as possible. The red panniers are almost out of sight by now.

On the outskirts of town we begin to climb a long hill, and the gap between us closes as my electric bike shows its muscle and begins to haul Terry in. At the crest of the hill I draw almost level with him and shriek at him to stop; over his shoulder he shouts something that is caught up and swept away by the noise of passing traffic. Again I yell, but he is unstoppable, inexorably rolling on like Ole Man River, while I bob along in his wake like a waterlogged paper boat. He turns onto a quiet lane winding through silent, dripping woods and zooms away down a steep hill. With all hope lost of being able to bring him to a halt, I have no choice but to follow, and we are travelling at exhilarating speed, slicing through the driving rain. My fingertips are a striking shade of mottled pink and purple and I'm virtually blinded by the rain on my glasses. It's terribly exciting and quite terrifying.

Shortly we arrive in Marnes-la-Coquette, a discreet village mid-way between Versailles and St Cloud. This is where the good, great and sufficiently wealthy have made their homes over the centuries. Surrounded by acres of park and woodland, it enjoys the highest per capita income in France. Napoléon III owned property there, and, seduced by the charms of the village known until then simply as Marnes, he added "la Coquette" (the Flirt) to its name, and the Imperial eagle to its coat of arms. Later Louis Pasteur used the same property as a centre for his research into rabies. This was not necessarily welcomed by the other residents of the village, who objected to the several dozen dogs, rabbits and guinea pigs housed in the grounds and destined for laboratory experiments. The snarling dog on the coat of arms is a tribute to Pasteur's successful development of a rabies vaccine. I had planned a surprise for Terry in Marnes-la-Coquette - a visit to the Escadrille Lafayette Memorial there in honour of the volunteer American airmen who had flown and died for France during WWI, before the United States entered the war. With their squadron insignia of a screaming native American Indian, and with two live lion cubs as their mascots, the wild bunch were heroic pioneers of aerial warfare, and I know that this is somewhere Terry, with his passion for military aviation, would find fascinating. However, he is always several yards ahead of me, pedalling as if our lives depend upon reaching an imaginary finishing line. Regardless of how hard I try, I cannot get close enough to signal him to stop; he cannot hear the pinging of my tinny bell, nor my frantic shrieking. The elegant bijou village is just a smudge on the landscape as we shoot into, through and out of it, missing not only the memorial, but also the turning to St Cloud that would lead us to the Bois de Boulogne. Instead we arrive in the centre of Sèvres, which is heavily congested with impatient traffic.

Sèvriens appear to have scant regard for cyclists, and try to kill us by a variety of methods: by turning abruptly across us in either direction without signalling, slamming on brakes with no warning, or opening their car doors just as we are drawing level with them. It is every man or woman for him or herself. There are multitudes of traffic lights, all of which change to red just as Terry hurtles through, leaving me on the wrong side and standing in the gutter inhaling fumes from revving engines. Terry's bike, like him, is quick and nimble. Mine is cumbersome and awkward, and unable to squeeze past the cars waiting at the lights, particularly as, tied to the baking tray that is tied to the luggage rack, are two sleeping bags and a rather wide tent which protrudes further than the handlebars. Each time the lights change to green, I have to wait for all cars to be clear before I move off, because until the bike gathers sufficient momentum, it wanders suicidally all over the road, and I do not want to be squashed without seeing Paris first.

The gap between us widens again, and although Terry looks back from time to time to check that I am still there, it does not cross his mind that I am following from necessity and not desire. We cannot afford to lose contact, firstly because Terry doesn't know which hotel I have booked in Paris, and secondly because I have no money on me. Without each other, we will be truly in the mire. Our one mobile phone is in Terry's jacket. There is no means of communication between us, so I grit my teeth and squeeze my elbows tighter into my ribs. The rain is harder now, dripping off my cycling helmet, running simultaneously down the back of my neck, and my face, and into the collar of my jacket. Still, this discomfort is forgotten because of what happens next: after a brief respite from traffic we are suddenly on a vehicle-infested dual carriageway, approaching a miniature Spaghetti Junction. Above us is a fly-over, supported on huge concrete pillars. We must turn left, across two lanes of fast traffic, filter into the path of thundering trucks coming from the right and make it across another two lanes of traffic coming from the left. This is so terrifying that I give up trying to think, and instead pedal mechanically, mindlessly, eyes fixed on the red panniers, and surprise myself by reaching the Pont de Sèvres intact. A Parisian contact from a cycling forum has warned me of the dangers of cycling on bridges, and recommended dismounting and pushing the bike over, which I do.

Terry has already reached the far end and at last has dismounted and is waiting for me. This is our first opportunity to speak to each other since leaving Versailles.

Wet, but clearly elated, he asks: "Well – how did you enjoy that?"

I am seething and shaking with inner fury, but do not wish to have a full-scale row in this public place nor at this early stage. "Not a great deal," I reply with what I consider great restraint. "I have been trying to ask you to stop since we left Versailles."

95

"I thought it was great!" he enthuses.

Yes, indeed, there are few things I enjoy as much as being concurrently cold, wet and frightened.

"Where do we go from here?" he asks.

"Through the Bois de Boulogne, up to the Arc de Triomphe, and then to our hotel near the Gare du Nord. And tomorrow morning, you'll have to go back and pick up the car. I'm not going to do this trip on a bike."

"What on earth are you saying?"

"Never mind for now, let's just get to the hotel and get ourselves warm and dry. We'll talk about it then."

PARIS

"The first thing that strikes a visitor to Paris is a taxi." Fred Allen, comedian

I take out the small folding map of Paris with all the cycling lanes marked on it and we follow the banks of the Seine until we can find an entrance into the Bois de Boulogne. Immediately I forget the horrors of the last couple of hours, because we have the whole beautiful park almost to ourselves. The only other wheeled vehicle we see is a pram pushed by a young woman; an occasional panting, chap-kneed jogger shuffles past. Twice we ride past Longchamps racecourse; several times we pass places that we have already passed. The map is no help and begins to dissolve. As lovely as the park is, cycling around it endlessly in rain begins to lose its appeal. As the racecourse comes into view yet again, we find a sad-faced man standing under a tree and ask him how to reach the Arc de Triomphe. He stares at us in astonishment, as if we were asking for directions to the lost city of Atlantis.

I repeat *"L'Arc de Triomphe."*

"L'Arc de Triomphe?" he echoes, his voice raised in bewilderment.

"Oui," I say, forcefully.

"But … it's a long way! At least two miles!"

Yes, but we are not ants. We are people on bicycles. Two, or even three miles is within even my meagre capabilities.

With obvious misgivings he points out a route, which we follow to a large roundabout, where the rain abruptly stops. Ahead of us the Avenue Foch glistens in pale sunshine. Diamond raindrops shimmer and drip from the trees lining the wide road, as if they are weeping for Napoléon, who would never march through the great triumphal arch, but instead would die in lonely exile. It's a shame about Waterloo, in a way. I feel sad for Boney.

Mixed with this sadness is great elation, because I have, against all my misgivings, cycled from Versailles to Paris, and am now standing, for the first time in my life, in the luminous city, just a few yards from one of its greatest landmarks. Little congratulatory tears spring to life and slither down my cheeks.

Our destination is a hotel of a slightly dubious reputation, but cheap, at the Gare du Nord, from which we are separated by the Arc de Triomphe and several miles of busy Parisian streets. With new-found and misplaced confidence I follow Terry as he happily plunges into the utter chaos of twelve roads heaving with traffic, all converging onto "*l'Étoile*" at 5.00 pm.

He instantly disappears between two trucks, and is swallowed up from sight, and I scream as a coach squeals to a halt in my path. Other cyclists whizz past. I am in a maelstrom of noise and vehicles, like a baby lamb in a Wild West show, straddling the bike and standing in the road, not knowing where to go next. I recall how all our French friends had reacted when we told them we would cycle through Paris. "But you will be crushed! It's too dangerous. You must not do it." I wish I'd taken them seriously, instead of shrugging them off in my most blasé manner and assuring them confidently that we English with our bulldog spirit were not easily deterred once we had made up our minds to do something.

Nobody seems to care that a woman and her bicycle are trapped and helpless amongst them; they weave around, glaring, blaring, or staring in disbelief. I turn the bike and drag it to a pavement. I start pushing it around the great circle, hoping that I will find Terry soon. He cycles up beside me, heedless of trucks and taxis and sightseeing buses, and commands that I mount my bike and just follow him, and I will be fine. But no thank you, I am content to plod along in a wide arc, heaving the bike up and down the kerbs, until reaching the Avenue de Friedland where there is a generous cycle lane painted onto the road.

Shaken, and a little stirred, I climb aboard and follow Terry, who is constantly waving his hands around pointing out interesting sights. I catch fragments of comments "…… fantastic …." "Did you ………?", but all my concentration is needed to keep inside the cycling lane and watch for the traffic lights. Sometimes I shout back "Yes, fabulous!" to be polite. I have assured him that if we keep cycling, sooner or later we'll see a sign for the Gare du Nord, and this is indeed what happens.

We cycle through the shopping mecca of Boulevard Haussman. Whilst Terry is goggle-eyed at the great department stores (I can only imagine this, as he is always several yards ahead of me, but I know his passion for shopping), I concentrate on cycling. My clearest vision of hell, after trying to cycle around the Arc de Triomphe at 5.00 pm on a Thursday evening, is traipsing around department stores. If I never had to buy another garment or piece of furniture for the rest of my life, that would be just fine by me.

Unlike dignified Boulevard Haussman, Rue La Fayette seems to be having a temper tantrum. Most likely this has been provoked by a series of diversions that have caused a total gridlock in the traffic. Nobody can go anywhere. Traffic lights might as well switch themselves off and go home, because nobody can obey them even if they wish to. Vehicles are bumper to bumper, and in one case a car has actually mounted the pavement in an effort to escape. Drivers are standing next to their cars, shouting and waving their arms around, or klaxoning each other. In this utter pandemonium, the pedestrian is king. Terry isn't doing too badly either, and has disappeared into the distance. There is no room to cycle in the road, because the vehicles are interlocked like pieces in a jigsaw puzzle. There is no way for me to thread my bike through them, so I heave it onto the pavement and use it as a battering ram against oncoming pedestrians, forcing some of them to allow me a little headway which otherwise they would not. When the end of the world arrives, this is how it will be, I imagine.

The red panniers are my beacon, guiding me through this mad chaos. When we eventually reach the Gare du Nord, the road is trembling beneath roaring machines gouging up the tarmac around the station. Temporary wooden walkways allow pedestrians to move from one place to another; however, they are rather narrow, with sharp bends around which it is impossible to steer a bicycle carrying a wide load such as mine, as I discover about half way along. This means wheeling the machine backwards, against the oncoming crowds, the most difficult challenge so far on this afternoon of trials. The pedestrians hurrying to catch trains are not impressed by my efforts, nor sympathetic to my dilemma.

Directly over the hotel's entrance - a narrow slot almost hidden between two cafés - dangles a menacing iron bucket full of chomped-up road surface. The machine to which it is attached growls and rattles, making conversation impossible. By grimacing and miming Terry and I agree that he will stand under the bucket with both bicycles while I go to check in and try to find somewhere to park them safely overnight.

As I walk into the lobby of the hotel, I am confronted by a weird, cartoon character. Legs encased in clinging black trousers, like Max Wall; upper half fighting to escape from a Lycra black and Day-glo green jacket; a round face, bright red and reflective with rivulets of perspiration running down it, crowned with a repulsive crimson cycling helmet. Betty Bumpkin, the cycling clown, I think as I stare at my reflection. What a holy mess. I cannot believe I look like this. I am truly aghast, and very angry at the hotel for placing a full-length mirror in such a thoughtless position. Before I knew what I looked like, I was relatively happy. Now I am utterly mortified, and forced to face several truths: not only am I a really crap cyclist. I need to lose weight. Skin-tight Lycra does not suit me. Neither does the helmet.

A smiling receptionist (I wonder, is he actually laughing, rather than smiling?) asks if he can be of help. I introduce myself and point to Terry and the bicycles, and ask if there is somewhere that we can safely leave them overnight. The receptionist, whose name is Ben, picks up a telephone – I hear the words "*anglais*" and "*bicyclettes*". With a dramatic flourish he replaces the receiver and announces that the *patron* is on his way, and will deal with the bicycles. Terry is impatient, and signalling to know why I am taking so long – it has been all of three minutes since I left him on the pavement. Ben skips up a very narrow winding staircase, beckoning me to follow. He flings open the door to a small room decorated in multi-shades of glowing orange. The effect is like being inside a carton of juice, but it is clean, dry and warm. Most importantly to me, there is a small wrought iron balcony overlooking the front of the historic Gare du Nord railway station. Ben shows me how to switch on the lights and plug in the television mounted on a bracket near the ceiling. He picks up the hairdryer from its pocket in the bathroom and points it at his head, making whooshing noises. No doubt my appearance has cast doubts as to my mental capacity.

Remembering my husband is still under the bucket, I thank Ben and spiral down the stairs, and find Terry playing an indignant tug-of-war with an elderly gentleman wearing carpet slippers. He has hold of my machine and is trying to push it across the road. Terry is trying to stop him from doing so. They are evenly matched: Terry is younger, but has to try and balance his own bike at the same time as tugging on to mine, as well as keeping in contact with all the bags and bundles he has unloaded onto the pavement. The two tuggers are talking to each other, each in a language that the other does not understand.

"This gentleman is trying to help," I explain to Terry. "He is the owner of the hotel. He is letting us put the bikes in his garage overnight." I introduce us both to his adversary, who has a small boy in tow, who politely shakes Terry's hand, and kisses me on both cheeks.

"Please, follow me." Leaving obliging Ben to carry the luggage up to our room, the *patron* ushers us over the road, waving a scornful hand at the diversions and diggers and wooden walkways.

"Terrible. No idea at all. London is much better, Mr. Livingstone knows what he's doing. Look what a terrible mess Delanoë," (the mayor of Paris) "is making. It was perfectly fine before he started playing about. Now see what's happened." The traffic is still at an effective standstill and the noise of drivers and vehicles is deafening.

Our new friend unlocks a metal grille beside a shop, and the door slides upwards at the top of a long steep slope leading to an underground car park. We have to lean back and dig in our heels to stop the bikes dragging us down. At floor number minus 2 he unlocks another metal door, and reveals a very large, powerful, expensive shiny motorbike that he pats and strokes lovingly.

"Is it yours?" Terry asks.

"Yes, of course. At the weekends I ride it out into the country."

It is an incongruous image, that of this stately and aged gentleman roaring around the French countryside astride a machine that looked more suited to a bearded, tattooed, horned-helmet Hell's Angel.

Once our bikes are stowed safely and locked up, we climb back up the long slope; Bertrand walks very slowly. He tells us that he is nearly 80, and has had a heart by-pass, and is not as fit as he used to be. He calls himself "Le Comte de Paris", he laughs, because his surname is Comte. He certainly has the aristocratic looks, bearing and manners to go with the title; he wishes us a happy evening as we part company.

Up in the radiant room we take it in turns to bathe, and then stand out on the balcony in the dusk. Now that the digging machines have closed down for the night, and their clanking, grinding noises are silenced, the traffic is no more than a rhythmic buzz, broken just once in a while by a brief peep, an occasional shout, a door closing. The streetlights awaken, illuminating the full havoc caused by the roadworks. We have an unhindered view of the magnificent Gare du Nord, an example of industrial design from an age when buildings were not only built for functionality, but also for beauty and elegance. Three tricolores flutter on the roof. The central elevation is topped by nine female statues, representing major international destinations.

At the next level down, and spanning the left and right flanks, sheltered in cosy niches are fourteen male statues dressed in flowing robes - they could be apostles, saints or kings, it is difficult to say - and they signify major French cities. To make it unmistakably clear which station this is, the word "Nord" is engraved in the stone eight times on the upper front elevation of the building, and again at ground-floor level. For good measure, "Chemin du Fer du Nord" is carved on the side of the wings.

Bertrand had mentioned that when the original station was completed in 1846 it was already too small to serve the booming railway traffic. It had been meticulously dismantled and transported to Lille where it is now known as the station of Lille Flandres. We are looking at La Gare du Nord mark II.

The station has always been a place of excitement and romance in my imagination, a haunt of spies, star-crossed lovers, and shadowy figures in long raincoats dragging on cigarettes and lurking with intent. We go to see if this bears any resemblance to reality, and I avoid looking in the cruel mirror in the lobby, because I really don't want to see what I look like in my little chiffon skirt and black top. Limited by the available space in our luggage, I team my "going out" wardrobe for the trip with a blue cycling jacket (to ward off the chilly evening air and scattered raindrops), and the gold moccasins which seemed the ideal footwear when I was packing, but look quite inappropriate now.

What is most noticeable about the concourse of the station is its cleanliness. The floors and the platforms shine as if they have been polished for hours. So do the trains standing with their noses buried in the colourful plants clambering from flowerboxes beneath the buffers. The half a million passengers who use the station daily haven't left any trace of their passing: not a sweet-wrapper, not a cigarette butt, not a dropped ticket in sight. With its shops and cafés and escalators the station resembles a skyport terminal, nothing like the vaguely sinister and murky sort of place I had imagined.

We decide to come back after we've eaten, when maybe the globe lights on their iron posts will add a romantic glow to the building, which the weak ambient light from the glass roof fails to do.

Multitudes of bars, *brasseries*, cafés and restaurants surround the station, and we select one where a lone waiter copes efficiently with a dozen tables and still manages a smile, and the food is fine.

Seen from a full stomach, half a bottle of rosé and two generous Baileys, in retrospect our journey today doesn't seem nearly as horrifying as it did when it was happening, and tomorrow there's only a short distance to negotiate before we will be out of town and into the countryside. I am pleased with myself for having come this far, and I realise that in some rather twisted way, I had quite enjoyed being terrified.

Even by lamplight, the interior of the Gare du Nord is too clean and bright to be romantic, and there are no signs of any shadowy figures or anguished lovers. Terry photographs a number of trains, until a burly, armed policeman politely stops him when he points his camera at the maroon and silver Thalys. The appeal of looking at trains has until now escaped me, but I cannot imagine that there exists a more exquisite engine that this svelte, bullet-shaped beauty that links Paris with Brussels, Amsterdam and Cologne.

"*Plan Vigipirate*," (France's anti-terror alert system) explains the *flic* [*French slang for a policeman*], a little apologetically.

When we arrive back at our hotel after 11.00 pm, Ben is still on duty, fresh as a daisy, and bright as a button. Breakfast, he explains, can be taken in our room, or in the cellar – he points down at the floor.

It takes me a long time to fall asleep because of the continual noise from the streets below, something I haven't heard for many years, living as we do in a small hamlet in the middle of rural France. Later, I wake disorientated, sure that we are in London and must get back to France as soon as possible. Terry reassures me that we are exactly where we are meant to be, and that I should go back to sleep.

VERSAILLES "Eat, drink and be merry, for tomorrow we die." Ecclesiastes 8:15

When some new friends, animal lovers, had volunteered to care for our menagerie for three weeks, we leapt at the rare opportunity to take a holiday. Two places we particularly wanted to visit were the palace of Versailles, and Epernay, the spiritual home of champagne. The two towns, roughly 150 miles distant from each other, are linked by the Marne valley, one of France's least publicised, yet most historic areas. Travelling by car is a poor way to get in touch with the countryside, and Terry didn't want to walk – a shame as walking is my major accomplishment. Ruling out boats, camels and horses as too expensive, impractical and restrictive, we had settled on cycling, albeit more than a little reluctantly on my part.

I still harbour bitter memories of the daily cycle ride to school when each new day, it seemed, brought a puncture, snatching brakes, snapping cables, or a greasy chain falling off and covering my legs with black marks. The bike was my enemy, making life as difficult, uncomfortable and dangerous as it could, and the prospect of riding one for several hundred miles was not one that filled me with extreme delight, but it would be the most practical way to travel, allowing us flexibility and the opportunity to enjoy and explore the countryside in a leisurely way. I'm a slothful creature with chronic back problems, and for the previous two years a trapped sciatic nerve had been causing unpredictable spasms of exquisite pain. To compensate for these personal shortcomings, I'd bought an electrically assisted machine. It wasn't a moped, it still needed to be pedalled, but the 36-volt battery delivered a fair boost, as if somebody was giving the bike a helping push, as my father had done when I was a small child. Managed carefully, a fully charged battery would last for up to 45 miles; all it needed was plugging into an electric power point for a few hours to recharge. Beginning at Versailles, after visiting the palace we'd cycle to Paris – a thought that I had pushed into the deepest recesses of my mind. From there we'd travel through the Marne *départément* in the Champagne-Ardennes region.

There seemed to be a dearth of information about the area; at the university library in Poitiers books about the Marne were remarkable for their non-existence on the shelves. The librarian searched her catalogue, to no avail. No, there wasn't a single publication dedicated to *département* 51. Our French friends pulled faces when we announced our plans to explore there, saying they were dubious that we'd find anything at all of interest.

While gathering information for our trip – something Terry was more than happy to leave to me – I noticed we would be following the same route as that taken by King Louis XVI and his Queen, Marie-Antoinette in their legendary attempt to escape from the wrath of the French Revolution. Where they had been, we were going, in their footsteps and wheel-tracks, and so I planned to try and integrate our journey with theirs.

With our bikes loaded onto the car, we drove to Versailles on the last day of May, a month that had been far from merry, each day having been uniformly grey and cold. That morning when we left home the skies had shown a promising hint of blue, but the nearer we came to Paris the gloomier appeared the clouds hanging over the capital. A few timid raindrops splattered onto the windscreen and by the time we arrived, Versailles was beneath a blanket of purple clouds and surrounded by rumbling thunder. We checked into our *chambre d'hôte*, swaddled ourselves in waterproofs, and cycled to the park, which we planned to explore today, visiting the palace tomorrow morning before leaving for Paris.

Five minutes later the clouds collapsed beneath their weight and exploded into a deluge, turning the roads into rivers and driving icy rain down the backs of our necks, up through our sleeves, and into our shoes. Together with a huddle of similarly soaked people we sought shelter in the nearest and only dry place, the park's lavatories, where a motherly lady promised that in a few minutes the sun would come bursting out. She was well meaning, but quite wrong. We stood eating a packet of miniature doughnuts while pebble-like raindrops battered the road and the cars parked along it. We discussed how we would cope if this weather lasted for the whole three weeks of our journey, as French friends had predicted it very likely would. Once the torrent had dwindled to a heavy drizzle, we rode around the park stoically, slashed by blades of freezing wind. I felt quite furious, absolutely enraged, that after an already overlong winter and dismal spring, the weather was still so disappointing on this, the last day of May, when it should have been at least spring-like, if not almost summery. After twenty minutes we admitted that we were not at all enjoying ourselves, so we changed our plans and went to visit the inside of the palace, queuing with a small group of other wet people waiting to get into the building that Marie-Antoinette had once so desperately wanted to get out of.

The palace peered out through a robust network of scaffolding that could not hide its vast splendour. When Louis XIV, the Sun King, disenchanted after five years of civil war, wished to relocate from Paris so that he could collect his devious aristocracy under one roof where he could keep an eye on them, he decided to transform his father's simple hunting lodge, known as the House of Cards, into the most legendary and opulent palace in the Western world. The cost was unimaginable. No expense was too great, neither in terms of money nor human life, for the solar monarch's self-glorification.

We began our visit in the chapel, an astonishing confection of gleaming gilt and bright white marble, sculpted stonework and fluted columns rising eighty feet to a vaulted and magnificently painted ceiling.

It was here that 14-year-old Austrian Archduchess Maria Antonia Josepha Joanna of Habsburg-Lorraine, more familiarly known now as Marie-Antoinette, took the first step towards the scaffold, when she married the lumpen 15-year-old French "dolphin" [*the hereditary title of the French heir apparent, dating back to the 11th century*], who would fairly soon have the misfortune of becoming Louis XVI of France.

If you believe in omens, you may find it significant that the Archduchess was born on the day following the cataclysmic Lisbon earthquake of 1755, which left an estimated 90,000 dead, and is still regarded as one of the world's most devastating natural disasters.

A high-spirited and poorly-educated tomboy, the young girl was a sacrificial offering made by her mother, Maria-Theresa, Archduchess, Queen of Austria and Holy Roman Empress, to preserve Franco-Austrian harmony. Despite maternal misgivings as to the future awaiting the girl, Maria-Theresa packed off her daughter to the French House of Bourbon, for what use were children if not to extend one's power base and protect one's borders? Anyway, she considered that her daughter should be more than satisfied to become a queen. Expecting happiness as well was just plain greedy.

It had taken many months for Austria and France to thrash out the fine points of the marriage contract between Louis and Marie-Antoinette, down to the most tedious of details. How many of this, how many of that; where, when, who, why and how. Protocol was everything. En route to her new life, the girl was ceremoniously handed over from Austria to France, and symbolically stripped of all her clothing, servants, pet dog, and even her name. From now on, she was exclusively French property.

Her bridegroom was dull, uncouth and most definitely not physically attractive; his interests were limited to hunting, fiddling with locks, and eating. He noted laconically in his diary, when his bride, having arrived in a great cavalcade, was introduced to him: "*Met the new wife.*" On his wedding day: "*My marriage. Apartment in the gallery. Royal banquet in the Salle d'Opera.*" A few days later: "*Had an indigestion.*" He could not be accused of being a romantic.

What were these two children, selected to be mated like animals, thinking about, I mused, during their marriage ceremony? Was Louis wondering how soon it would be over so that he could go hunting? Was the bride missing her mother and siblings?

To celebrate the royal marriage, a grand firework display was held at the square called Place Louis XIV in Paris. A fire broke out; the crowd stampeded to escape the flames, and 132 people were trampled to death.

Another bad omen? Twenty-two years later, that square would have been renamed Place de la Revolution. It was the last place the newly-weds would ever see.

But let's not worry too much about that just now. It's a long way off, and we have far to go.

From the chapel we trundled on along with the crowd from one gold-plated room to the next. There was not a square inch of floor, wall or ceiling that was not ornately adorned. It looked to me (and I have to admit that unlike Terry, I am not a lover of fancy furnishings, frills and flounces,) as if successive inhabitants had tried to see just how much decoration they could cram into the available space. From one room to another we all shuffled, past marble pillars, gilded doors; glittering chandeliers, polished candelabras and porcelain jars; bronze busts, oil paintings, marble sculptures, mirrors, tapestries, vases, chairs and sofas that looked uncomfortable, and ugly, heavy cabinets and tables with hard edges. Very bad Feng Shui. We gawped at painted ceilings until our necks ached. Overwhelming opulence, wild profligacy, the triumph of excess over moderation, it seemed to me a beautiful example of more is never enough.

The air smelt of damp clothing and hair, and chewing gum, but it was not offensive. During the 18th century, for all its splendour, one thing had been notable for its absence - proper sanitation. In the absence of lavatories, people answered the call of nature wherever they happened to be at the time the need arrived, both outside and inside the château, and the stench of urine and human faeces pervaded the air.

Ahead of us a band of solemn Japanese tourists listened intently to a gentleman holding a microphone and waving a bright orange flag on a long stick, as he shepherded them from room to room. Behind us a group of giggling American teenage girls seemed more interested in sending text messages than looking at the rooms and their contents. They would have been about the same age as the young Archduchess when she arrived at Versailles, and I wondered how any one of them would have reacted if she had been told that she was to be married to somebody she had never met, and who had neither good looks nor charm but with whom she would be obliged to share a bed and produce children. I doubt that any of these young American girls came from a particularly affluent or powerful family, but each of them would certainly have more control over their own destiny than the unlucky, beautiful and rich little girl whose scheming mother was one of the most powerful women in the Western world. Those were my thoughts as I watched the girls nudging each other, whispering behind their hands, and sharing photos on their mobile phones.

Where life at court in her native Austria had been relaxed and informal, and morals were strict, in contrast at Versailles etiquette ruled and morals were almost non-existent. Combined with the stifling, small-minded formality of the 17th century French court where a misplaced step in the minuet was cause for gasps and gossip, I thought that living in the palace of Versailles must have felt like being imprisoned in a constantly turning kaleidoscope.

The teenage Archduchess was entrusted to a lady of great virtue with an impeccable knowledge of court protocol. Her task was to ensure that the new arrival understood exactly what to do, when, how, where, and with and to whom. Nothing must be left to chance – a headdress worn at the wrong angle was sufficiently scandalous to provoke a fainting fit.

The Dauphine's day was occupied by prayers, rituals of dressing and having her hair dressed in public, more prayers, visits with Royal family members - in particular her aunts (the granddaughters of Louis XV), dining in public, needlework, music lessons, more family visits, reaching a crescendo of excitement with late night games of cards. A particular trial was the custom of dining in front of an audience of people who came to Versailles specifically to watch the royals eat. While her husband could nonchalantly demolish as many dishes as were put before him, and his grandfather had delighted spectators by his skill at decapitating his egg with a single swipe of his fork, the new Dauphine must have made for poor entertainment, as she had a modest appetite, and washed her simple meals down with water.

Louis XV gave his granddaughters - the Dauphin's aunts - affectionate nicknames: Pig, Tatters, Mite, and Rubbish. Madame Campan, Marie-Antoinette's first lady of the bedchamber, describes Sophie, aka Mite, as a person of the most unprepossessing appearance: "...*she walked with the greatest rapidity; and, in order to recognise the people who placed themselves along her path without looking at them, she acquired the habit of leering on one side, like a hare.*"

Louise (Rubbish) moved into a Carmelite convent and became a nun.

A disinterested and gauche young husband, a licentious grandfather-in-law, four odd aunts and a strict disciplinarian guardian: what fun it must have not been.

Amongst the gilt and gloss and glitz of this museum I had difficulty in imagining it as a home, where men and women had lived and loved and schemed and dreamed and worked and died, and looked out of the same windows that we were looking out of, at the same views. What stories the walls could tell, if only ....

Contemporaneous accounts suggest that despite her youth, the new bride could be a bit of a handful when she chose. Until her arrival, the King's powerful mistress, Madame du Barry, had been the undisputed Queen Bee at Versailles. As a commoner, and in Marie Antoinette's eyes no better than she ought to be, etiquette decreed that the du Barry could not address her until she was invited to do so. Marie-Antoinette took it into her teenage head that she would not speak to the royal favourite. Du Barry waited; the King waited, the whole court waited for the necessary invitation; the King used all his powers of persuasion in various quarters, and the du Barry all but turned herself inside out in her efforts to win her over, but Marie-Antoinette continued to ignore her. Her stubborn refusal threatened to have serious consequences far beyond the walls of Versailles, reaching into the intricacies and intrigues of Eastern European politics. As Russia, Prussia and Austria were busily dividing Poland between themselves, the Polish king was appealing to the Western European powers for help. The last thing that the Dauphine's mother, Empress Maria-Theresa of Austria needed was for the

French to go to war on behalf of Poland. But the King was becoming increasingly angry and losing patience with his daughter-in-law; who knew what the repercussions might be. Maria-Theresa wrote to her daughter in such forceful terms that the girl finally agreed to bend her neck.

"*There are a lot of people at Versailles today,*" she said, addressing the du Barry for the first and very last time. Those few words represented a victory for the King's mistress, a defeat for the Dauphine, a source of mixed delight and disappointment for the Court, according to whose side they had supported, and they sealed Poland's fate.

While the young couple were still in their teens, Louis XV contracted smallpox, and was dying a gruesome death - "*the whole surface of his body coming off piecemeal and corrupted*" was the unpleasantly graphic description by contemporary historian, Jean-Louis Soulavie. The King's priests would neither receive his confession nor administer the last rites as long as his mistress was living under the roof of the palace. So Madame du Barry was bundled off, and the King mercifully died, in a state of grace and decomposition. It was customary for monarchs to be embalmed, but the chief surgeon was not prepared to risk his own certain death by fiddling with the infectious remains; when ordered to do so by the First Gentleman of the King's bedchamber, the surgeon responded that he would obey if the First Gentleman would hold the royal head, as his position required him to do. The matter was dropped, and the defunct monarch quickly whisked away for burial without any of the usual pomp, leaving two mismatched adolescents the new King and Queen of France and heralding the promise of a new golden age under the reign of Louis XVI.

We arrived at Marie-Antoinette's bedroom, which is sandwiched between a dining room and a gaming room. Whether it was always so, I've no idea. Seems a bit odd. But in any case she enjoyed very little privacy, even in her own bed. Each day when she woke it was to a room full of courtiers elbowing each other aside for her attention as she performed her toilette. It was the privilege of the highest-ranking lady present to help the Queen into such items of clothing as she chose from a gold or silver tray. Should a lady of superior rank arrive during the dressing ceremony, then she would take control of the garment, while the Queen had to wait patiently for it to change hands until it reached her so that she could finish dressing. To preserve her modesty when bathing, she wore a flannel gown that enclosed her from neck to ankles; and with the same modesty she went to bed wearing beribboned corsets with lace sleeves.

There was no privacy, either, in the very depths of the intimate lives of the royal couple. Marie Antoinette had not been given to France as an ornament. Her function was to produce an heir, something that required the active participation of both parties; but Louis didn't appear to be active; or if he was, he was not effective, and no fruit was forthcoming to add to the family tree. Spiteful courtiers pointed cruel accusatory fingers at the young bride. It was plainly her fault. Despite her best efforts, and the explicit advice given to her in letters from her mother, the future Queen was still a virgin seven years after her marriage. Her sex life was public property, openly discussed by family, friends, foes, foreign ambassadors and the ladies of the bedchamber, right down to the lowliest washerwomen. Everybody knew that the marriage had not been consummated. Differing explanations were given for this unsatisfactory situation, depending upon who was doing the explaining. Either it was a small irregularity in Louis' equipment, which needed a minor operation to enable him to function, or it was a serious disproportion between the couple that made the process too painful. Whichever it was, once things were finally working correctly, Louis confided in one of his aunts that he had discovered a source of very great pleasure, and regretted that it had taken him so long to do so. It seems somewhat unusual that a young man should discuss his sex life with a maiden aunt, but anyway, it's good to know that he enjoyed his marital obligations. We don't know whether his wife shared his enthusiasm, but she certainly did look forward to having children, and had sometimes wept in private over her inability to become a mother whilst her sisters and sisters-in-law were regularly churning out infants.

Of the crosses she had to bear, surely the Queen's domineering mother must have been one of the heaviest. During the first seven barren years of her marriage, she had not only to endure the contempt and disappointment of France, but also relentless pressure and advice from her mother, who had casually produced a litter of sixteen little Archdukes and Archduchesses. Each month, the unfortunate girl wrote to her mother, apologising that she could not give her the news she wanted. Each month, her fecund parent wrote back with admonishments and advice as to how her daughter should behave in the bedroom. Unlike her daughter, Maria Theresa was fortunate enough to have been in love with her husband, so she would not have known what it was like to have to regularly climb into bed with somebody with whom she had nothing in common, purely for the purpose of procreating.

His mother-in-law strongly disapproved of Louis' preference for sleeping alone. She disapproved of him tiring himself out hunting, and prayed that bad weather would keep him indoors. She disapproved of her daughter staying up late at night gambling. And she never hesitated to express her disapproval in her endless nagging letters. Even after the birth of Marie-Antoinette's first child, a daughter, the bombardment of letters kept on coming.

"*We must have a Dauphin!*" wrote Maria Theresa in June 1780.

In August 1780 again she wrote: "*We must have a Dauphin!*"

It is an indication of the obedient and good-natured character of her daughter that she wrote to "*Madame ma très chère mère*," with never-failing politeness and patience. A less dutiful daughter might well have written: "OK, mother. You're the expert. You come and do it."

Once her royal spouse had mastered the necessary technique, over the following eight years Marie-Antoinette became dutifully pregnant five times, and produced four live children.

By tradition, royal mothers gave birth in public, and when the Queen went into labour for the first time in December of 1778 it was in front of a huge and motley crowd who rushed into the bedroom, clambering on top of the furniture in their

113

determination not to miss an exciting moment of the spectacle. Producing a baby whilst surrounded by such a commotion caused the Queen to develop life-threatening symptoms, and she had to be bled.

And after all that, it was only a daughter.

By an unkind stroke of fate her manipulative mother died three years later. Only thirteen months after her death, Marie-Antoinette triumphantly produced a son, the new Dauphin, who would, if things had worked out differently, have one day become Louis XVII of France. The King mentioned "my son, the Dauphin" at every opportunity, and there was jubilation throughout the land, although it was not shared by either of Louis' two younger brothers. Charles-Philippe, the Comte d'Artois, and the Comte de Provence, also confusingly named Louis, had both been rather hoping to have the crown for themselves.

Marie-Antoinette was a loving and devoted mother, set on bringing up her children sensibly, outside the rigid royal protocol. After the arrival of her first baby, she wrote to her mother:

"The way children are raised now, they are much less fussed over. They are not wrapped up the moment they can go outside, and, as they gradually become accustomed to it, they end up spending most of the time there. I think it is the best and the healthiest way to raise them. My child will stay downstairs, with a little barrier that will separate her from the rest of the terrace, where she can also learn to walk sooner than she would on the parquet floors." [Madame Campan, "Memoirs of the Private Life of Marie Antoinette".]

We shuffled on to the Hall of Mirrors, which was in the throes of restoration, but even with only half of it visible, this room sparkled. In Elisabeth Feydeau's book "The Scented Palace", she describes the weird colours which were created for fabrics during Marie-Antoinette's reign: "flea" which came in shades of young, old, belly, back and leg. Face powders bore names like "Dauphin's poo" and "Goose-shit". Beauty spots shaped like stars, crescents or hearts were used to signal the mood of the wearer depending on whereabouts they were placed, or alternatively used to cover up a "sapphire", more commonly known as a pimple. Like peacocks the men and women of the court minced around, prancing and preening themselves. Hairdressers created ever more bizarre styles: towering structures stuffed with fruits, vegetables and flowers, birds, ships, dolls, ribbons, feathers and ornaments. Hats and hairstyles became so tall that the wearers could no longer travel in their carriages without either kneeling on the floor, or having the seats lowered. People lived to show off and out-do one another, and the Hall of Mirrors provided the ideal setting for them to do so and to admire themselves.

To do justice to this extravaganza of extravagance of a room, it called for men in high-heels, curly wigs and hats crowned with feathers; ladies with powdered white skin and rouged cheeks, in big dresses with their bosoms spilling out; pet monkeys and peacocks, whispers and laughs, sly looks and fluttered eyelashes; it needed liveried flunkies carrying pyramids of exotic fruits, *petits fours* and *bonnes bouches* on golden platters; hothouse plants and rival scents. It needed lapdogs and hunting dogs, swords and beauty patches, baroque music, jewelled fans, and sycophants. Today's throng of scruffy 21st century tourists wearing woolly hats, backpacks, cameras, anoraks and open mouths, and a woman in Lycra with purple hair didn't quite work.

In the Coronation Room we relished David's enormous painting of Napoléon's coronation. The artist had captured every sour and indignant line on the face of Pope Pius as the Emperor, already crowned by his own hand, places the crown on Josephine's head. His message was clear: there is only one top dog here, and it isn't the Pope.

The Hall of Battles was exactly that: one giant canvas after another depicting victorious French generals and armies engaged in battle with their neighbours. There may well have been some French defeats shown too, but there were so many paintings, and all of them such a mêlée of limbs, weapons and animals that it was difficult to see who was winning, and our fellow visitors stood in the way of the captions that might have enlightened us.

Not everybody who had lived at Versailles had done so in comfort or elegance. Some nobles had to make do with attics, but luckily a tour of these was not included in the cost of our tickets.

Neither did I want to visit any more royal apartments. After admiring four or five rooms, I had already seen enough for one day, or possibly for a lifetime. The more I saw, the more I found them oppressive and suffocating. The concept of "Less is more" had certainly not intruded into Versailles.

Ranks of busts of French notables gazed blindly down their proud marble noses as we made our way to the exit. Terry, who loves ornate decoration and furnishings, said he thought the palace of Versailles was magnificent, and was already suggesting new decorating ideas for our house. My choice leans more towards plain white walls and functional furniture that doesn't collect dust, and although I could appreciate the craftsmanship that had gone into the palace, I was relieved to get out into the uncomplicated cold grey air and pelting rain.

By the time we had cycled back to our *chambre d'hôte* we were saturated, and blue with cold. Watching the storm lashing against the windows that rattled with every crash of thunder, I felt vindicated and justified at having baulked at the exorbitant fees charged by the local camp site, opting instead for this dry, warm room where we could soak away the misery of the weather in a good deep bath.

Swathed in grey gloom, the town of Versailles felt to me as if, after the beleaguered royals had been frog-marched off to the capital in 1789 by the Parisian fish-wives, the town had decided that it had seen enough excitement to last for the foreseeable future, and beyond, and now wished for nothing more than to sink into obscurity, peace and quiet.

For dinner we went to a piano-bar restaurant that advertised live music. When we were quite well into our meal, and no piano player had appeared, I asked our waiter what time we could expect this to happen. Apparently we could not, as we had chosen one of the rare nights when there was no live piano, but instead taped music – Michael Jackson, Zucchero, Garou; not exactly what we were expecting, but nevertheless very much to my taste, and acceptable to Terry. Simultaneously a large television, suspended from the ceiling, with the sound turned off, was showing an old black and white documentary about the development of jazz, jive and jitterbug. Watching the one, while listening to the other, was really a rather surreal experience, with its total lack of synchronisation of movement and sound.

A group of eight people at a table nearby were holding a meeting of some kind, dominated by one man with a very loud voice and strong opinions that he emphasised by standing up and flailing his arms around. He was either oblivious of, or indifferent to the fact that he was in a restaurant where people were trying to enjoy a meal, and the obvious frustration of his colleagues who were cut off in mid-sentence each time one of them tried to speak. Several times they gathered together their papers and stood up as if ready to leave, but were compelled to sit down again by the sheer force of his personality. Between the sound of the music, the jerky black and white images and the loud man, the atmosphere in the piano bar was not at all what we had anticipated, but the food and service were fine. Although we had only arrived in Versailles at 3.00 pm that afternoon, it felt as if we had packed quite a lot into the last seven hours.

Small is Beautiful – Less Is More
"Have nothing in your houses that you do not know to be useful or believe to be beautiful." **William Morris**

We woke to brilliant sunshine, and went to the long-term underground car park to arrange to leave our car for the three weeks we'd be away. The manager went to great lengths explaining the procedure for using the ticket, and the benefits it would heap upon us. He printed out an invoice, then a receipt, and then a ticket, and showed us how to put the ticket into the machine. Whether it was because we looked particularly witless, or because we were English and he suspected we might be fools too, he showed us again, just to make sure that we understood. He was absolutely charming and very handsome, and I said "You look very much like ..." but before I could finish he laughed and said: "Yes, I know, Zinedine Zidane – everybody tells me that."

While I was assuring him that we wouldn't lose the ticket, understood the repercussions if we did, and would remember how to use it, and thanking him for all his help, Terry had unearthed an exciting discovery in an underground workshop that

117

was part of the garage: twelve Ferraris being overhauled. It isn't often you see a dozen Ferraris together. I think that for him this was probably the highlight of our visit to Versailles.

In a cheerful mood induced by the change in the weather, we packed our belongings carefully and cycled back to the park of Versailles. With our record of nearly always arriving at places when they are closed, we should not have been surprised that just as the palace was in the throes of renovation, so too were the gardens. All the ponds and fountains were empty; heavy machinery was digging up channels and laying new pipes, and there were mounds of muddy earth all over the place. There was nothing in bloom, and everything was either green, or path-coloured. We roamed around the gardens of the palace, down the side of the Grand Canal, along the endless, perfectly hedged lanes, and through dozens of groves with their statues and empty ornamental ponds. Considering that the Sun King had enlarged his palace and herded his nobles under its roof so that he could keep his eye on them and nip in the bud any potential treachery, it seemed strange to me that there were so very many secluded places in the grounds where people so inclined could meet in secrecy. The labyrinthine layout was a perfect milieu for intrigue and clandestine encounters. If I had been in his high-heeled, beribboned shoes, I'd have had the whole place dug up and lawned so that nobody had anywhere to hide.

As a wedding gift, young Louis gave Marie-Antoinette the little palace known as Le Petit Trianon originally built for Madame de Pompadour by Louis XV. Dignified, elegant and small enough to be homely, it became the Queen's refuge from the tiresome etiquette demanded at court. A sanctuary where she could let down her hair, kick off her shoes and entertain her friends.

Madame Campan describes in her "Memoirs of the Private Life of Marie-Antoinette," the relaxed lifestyle enjoyed by everybody at the Petit Trianon, where admission was strictly by invitation of the Queen, and where she and her close friends amused themselves with games or pastimes.

"There was but little room in the small château of Trianon. Madame Elisabeth" (the King's sister) *"accompanied the Queen there, but the ladies of*

honour and ladies of the palace had no establishment at Trianon. When invited by the Queen, they came from Versailles to dinner. The King and Princes came regularly to sup. A white gown, a gauze kerchief, and a straw hat were the uniform dress of the Princesses."

Madame Campan continues that although the Queen was notorious for her extravagance, this was unwarranted and she could in fact be rather stingy.

"...she amused herself with improving the gardens, without allowing any addition to the building, or any change in the furniture, which was very shabby, and remained, in 1789, in the same state as during the reign of Louis XV. Everything there, without exception, was preserved; and the Queen slept in a faded bed, which had been used by the Comtesse du Barry. The charge of extravagance, generally made against the Queen, is the most unaccountable of all the popular errors respecting her character. She had exactly the contrary failing; and I could prove that she often carried her economy to a degree of parsimony actually blameable, especially in a sovereign."

I don't know how many of the current materials in Petit Trianon are original, as the building had just undergone extensive renovations, but as we walked up the marble steps of the staircase, I wondered whose feet had trodden there, and whose hands had touched the black and gold stair rail. Had Marie Antoinette, and later Napoléon, looked out of the same window to admire the colourful flowery gardens behind the house, just as we were doing? I put a light fingertip on a marble fireplace, in case one of them had previously touched it. "*Ne touchez pas!*" snapped an officious girl sitting in the corner on a chair. Too late, I already had.

Of Marie-Antoinette and Louis' marriage, Stefan Zweig, in his book '*Marie-Antoinette – Portrait of an Average Woman*' (Grove, 2002) says that despite the fact that the couple were absolute opposites in all respects, their union was a happy one. Louis was not physically attractive, nor quick-witted or extrovert, but he was well read, courteous and kind, and paid his wife's bills. She dutifully produced four children for him, and to them he was a doting father. According to a letter written by her brother, the Emperor of Austria, she felt that after producing four children she had sufficiently fulfilled her obligations to France in the matrimonial bed and wished to be allowed to withdraw from it.

There has always been speculation as to whether or not Marie-Antoinette had an affair with the handsome Swedish diplomat Axel Fersen. She had long been accused by her enemies of infidelity, lesbianism and all manner of depravity; she might as well have been hung for a sheep as a lamb. Whether or not their relationship was more than platonic we will probably never know. We do know though, from letters that remain, that they were in love, but beyond that there is only conjecture. Madame Campan, like the loyal servant she was, never mentions their relationship. It doesn't seem that Louis was unduly disturbed by her retreat from his bed, and there is no record of him ever having any sort of involvement with another woman. I hope that the Queen did enjoy some boudoir pleasures with Fersen, in recompense for her dutiful coupling with Louis, so that she had at least some sweet memories during her future ordeal. That's what was going through my mind as we stood in the bedroom, looking at the exquisite, very small bed.

Originally the Petit Trianon garden comprised formal flowerbeds and massive, expensive hot houses where exotic plants and fruits grew. Under Marie-Antoinette's ownership up, down and out these were ripped, to be replaced with a bucolic landscape of a wiggling stream, lakes, waterfalls and grottoes, arbours and follies, meadows of wild flowers and beautiful specimen trees; a transformation to the simplicity which she craved but which, ironically, was only achieved at scandalous expense.

We followed a pathway towards the Queen's little hamlet, past a very ordinary tortoiseshell cat with a red collar curled up beneath a shrub, watching us through slitted eyes with a rather smug expression.

Whilst we were walking around the quaint collection of timbered, thatched cottages where the Queen used to entertain herself pretending to be a milkmaid or shepherdess, a group of 6-year-old French schoolgirls surrounded Terry, jumping about and asking him questions in fractured English. He hadn't very much idea what they were saying, and they could barely understand a word he said, so each exchange sent them into an eruption of giggles. When their teachers ushered them away, they queued up to kiss Terry's cheek, then skipped away, stopping once or twice to wave at him, leaving him flattered and quite bemused. French children can be so enchanting.

In June of 1787 the royal parents lost their youngest child, baby Sophie-Beatrix, just before her first birthday. Almost exactly two years later they were mourning the death from tuberculosis of their eldest son, the seven-year-old Dauphin Louis-Joseph, frail, crippled and deformed. In her private letters, Marie-Antoinette had expressed her hopes and fears for the ailing child. He was a little better, the fever had left him. Maybe it was only teething that was making him so ill. The physicians were worried again. The little boy had been moved to the château at Meudon, where his father, as a sickly child, had profited from the cleaner air – and just look what a strapping chap he had become. Louis-Joseph seems much improved. He is giving cause for alarm. The physicians don't believe he will last the night, but he rallies. The next day the little boy they had tried for so long to produce, and of whom they were so proud, dies.

Maybe the couple were so wrapped in grief that they failed to recognise the gravity of the situation as the political crisis that had long been brewing in France neared its zenith. Maybe that's why Louis hunted and Marie-Antoinette played at being a peasant in her twee hamlet. But all the while she was living her rural idyll, or treading the boards in her private theatre, and Louis was galloping around killing wildlife, the common people of France were getting increasingly hungry, and very angry. They stormed the Bastille. But in the palace of Versailles, nobody took much notice.

Nineteen years after Marie Antoinette's triumphant arrival to marry the Dauphin, a furious and vicious mob of knife-wielding harridans, several thousand strong, surrounded the royal family and those faithful friends who had remained with them at Versailles, and forcibly marched them off to Paris. The King and Queen would not see Versailles ever again.

The morning was drifting away. We had to cycle to Paris that afternoon, so we began making our way back through the gardens to our chambre d'hôte to collect our luggage. As we passed the lake a shoal of carp, each large enough to make a meal for six people, surged through the water towards us and poked their heads up, opening and closing their mouths silently, plainly saying "Feed us." They followed us hopefully around the edge of the water, until they spotted some more people arriving, and splashed away to try their chances with them.

We stopped in one of the glades at a place selling drinks and fast-food snacks, and ordered a couple of coffees from a softly spoken, smiling black man. While he was preparing them, an American customer came up to the counter and queried his bill – he thought he'd been overcharged. The black man listened politely, opened and checked the till, apologised to the customer and handed him a few coins. A swarthy man in a camouflage jacket, matching trousers tucked into black boots, and very dark glasses appeared from behind some shelves, and harangued the black man loudly. Although we were embarrassed, the man himself seemed quite composed and after a few minutes wandered off to chat to another swarthy person also dressed in para-military clothing. When we stood up to leave, that person yelled "Oi!" and pointed at the two plastic cups we had left on the table, and told us rudely to put them into the bin. He could have taken four steps and put them there himself, if he unglued himself from the wall against which he was lolling. Giving Terry an order is tantamount to tweaking Mike Tyson's nose and asking him what he's going to do about it. Before he had time to react, I picked up the cups and threw them into the bin: the swarthy man looked as if he was hoping for an excuse to pull out an Uzi and blow us away.

It left us wondering whether visitors to Versailles deserved mediocre refreshments from an enterprise that appeared to be run by some sort of Eastern European mafia who were rude to their staff and customers. Do pizza and Coke and plastic cups fit into the fabled sophistication of the place? Should there not be tisanes, infusions, hot chocolate and delicate savouries and pastries served by demure French wenches in Bo-Peep costumes, or deferential flunkeys in frogged livery?

By early afternoon we'd seen as much as we wanted, and the weather looked to be deteriorating, so after loading our bikes we had set off on the hair-raising ride to our hotel in Paris. I doubted that Marie-Antoinette could have been more terrified on her final journey from Versailles to the capital than I was on this, my first.

Extract from *'The Valley Of Heaven and Hell - Cycling In The Shadow Of Marie Antoinette'* by Susie Kelly

For links to Amazon Kindle USA, Amazon Kindle UK & Paperback sales pages please go to
http://blackbird-digitalbooks.com

and click on the book cover.

5
SWALLOWS & ROBINS
The Guests In My Garden

As the world's worst housekeeper, running holiday homes wasn't, with hindsight, a sensible idea. But two collapsing buildings on Susie Kelly's land would cost more to demolish than to restore. Thus she became a seasonal landlady and, along with the assorted guests, came Ivy into her life, The Cleaning Lady From Hell.

Our Uncle Charlie was a dapper little man who lived with his cat, Tibbles, in a decaying but very large house in a less desirable area of London. Bought for £350 ($570) during the 1960s, despite its current condition and location the property had increased manifold in value and was worth a handsome sum of which we had been allocated a generous portion "when the time came".

Uncle Charlie had not always been little, but he had always been dapper. He was proud of his wartime service as a rear gunner on Lancaster bombers. Several photographs showed a sturdy, fresh-faced fellow in his RAF uniform and later in his demob suit. They bore no discernible similarity to the shrunken body and shiny head sitting in the armchair he had bought in 1956. Tibbles was the beneficiary of all the devotion and admiration that Uncle Charlie had once given to his wife, who had died twenty years previously and whom everybody who knew her agreed had been a spiteful cow. He was passionately supportive of Tottenham Hotspur football club, and anxious that when he passed through his own heavenly goalposts his wealth should be well and wisely spent.

Each time we visited Uncle Charlie his clothes looked another size too large, but his shirt was still crisp and white, his tie perfectly knotted, and his blazer buttons polished.

"Promise me," he said, reaching out with a clawed little hand, "promise you won't go frittering it away when I'm gone. Use it for something sensible."

We promised.

Eventually Uncle Charlie became so small that he simply vanished, leaving behind a small rectangular hump of earth, two tiny bunches of flowers, and the pot of money which we were honour bound to spend sensibly.

Up there on his celestial cloud, would Uncle Charlie regard a six-month world cruise as a sensible investment? It would broaden our horizons, allow us to visit new places, meet new people, learn new cultures, eat good food and not have to do anything demanding or energetic. It was almost certain that we would never again have such an opportunity.

On the other hand two ancient buildings on our property, originally houses, latterly used as a garage and stable, currently occupied by various wildlife, were falling down. Decades of frost, wind and rainfall had toppled the chimneys. The roofs had caved in, the walls were cracking apart, and the rain was flushing away the mud and animal muck that precariously held the remaining stones in place. Soon they would be reduced to piles of rubble to be removed at vast expense.

So the cruise was off. Instead of travelling around the world meeting new people, they would be coming to us, bringing with them their hopes, habits, hang-ups and idiosyncrasies. Many became friends for life. Some came and went almost unnoticed. Others left lasting impressions. Terry, my husband, has always said that I am like a magnet for crackpots, and certainly a number of them managed to make their way here. Meet the swallows and robins – our summer and winter visitors. At the time there were some whom I could have happily battered to bits with a shovel, but now, after many years have passed I can look back on them all, perhaps ruefully, but certainly with affection.

Year One – First Find Your Builder

The work required to convert the buildings is enormous, and our inheritance will have to be managed with atomic precision. Artisan builders are beyond our means. We must put our trust and money into a one-man, jack-of-all-trades outfit. The saying about peanuts and monkeys rings in my ears.

Living here on my own for much of the time, while Terry works in England, the responsibility for organising and feeding the monkey rests on me, and I admit that I am daunted. I've heard terrible stories about builders. I don't like fights, shouting, threats, aggravation of any kind and will go to considerable lengths to avoid it. I will willingly drive back and forth to builders' merchants for sacks of cement, timber and any other materials; within the limits of my physical strength I will hold, lug and lift things. I will supply tea and/or coffee willingly, and in copious amounts, and I will pay, promptly, the agreed number of peanuts. In return I will not expect miracles, but an honest day's work, each and every day, resulting in two habitable buildings.

Some friends have recommended a retired French stonemason who can also turn his hand to roofing. He arrives by moped, with a ragged cigarette clenched between his lips. He is very tiny like a marmoset, with round, rheumy eyes and tufts of hair burgeoning from his ears and nose. He is surprisingly strong for his size, and agile for his age. He heaves stones and timbers, and shovels rubble into wheelbarrows; his friend comes and takes away the rubble in a trailer. At exactly 12 noon each day, the marmoset lays down his tools and takes out from his overall an Opinel knife, and from a box on his moped an evil-smelling garlic sausage, a baguette and a bottle of red wine. He sits down on a bench in the garden, munches methodically, drinks the bottle of wine, accepts a small cup of black coffee, comments on the weather, disappears to the end of the field behind a hedge, and at precisely 1.30 pm is back at work. By the end of the first week reusable stones and timbers are neatly stacked, and most of the rubble has gone. Maurice the marmoset is polite, respectful, knows what he's doing and gets on and does it. What more could we want?

He doesn't arrive on Monday morning of the second week, and his telephone is unanswered. Late in the afternoon his friend comes to say that Maurice has fallen off his moped and broken two fingers. He will not be able to continue working. This is a real blow. The friend cannot recommend anybody else to take his place.

I search for a new monkey. One wants too many peanuts, and one cannot start for at least two months. That only leaves a stubbly-jawed, stocky fellow with muscles and an insolent attitude. He starts his working day with a picnic in the back of his old van, drinking half of a bottle of red wine and eating a tin of sardines. At noon, he finishes the bottle and chops chunks of cheese onto a baguette. By early afternoon his breath can kill at fifty paces. Like Maurice he's a good worker, but he has several times referred to my "*belles fesses*," and when I look it up in the dictionary I find it means nice bum. It is only a matter of time – three days to be precise – before he lunges at me, pins me to a wall and nearly suffocates me with his toxic breath. I shout to the dogs – we have five and he is nervous of them – and when I have re-established my composure I pay him off.

Next is an English jack-of-all trades who promises much. After two days, even as a novice myself I can see that he is out of his depth and doesn't know where to start or what to do. He sits in the garden and makes lists and orders materials and sketches plans and drinks litres of coffee, but after two weeks nothing much has changed. There are piles of materials all over the place and two windows put into the upstairs of the larger cottage. Something about them doesn't look right, but I can't put my finger on exactly what. He had promised the properties would both be ready by mid-July – that's in four months' time. Now he is talking of "trying to get one ready this year, and finishing the other next year."

I am a failure as a project manager/monkey handler. Paying Jack-of-all-trades his weekly peanut ration hurts, because he is not earning it. My neighbour tells me that if I go out, Jack sits in the garden sunbathing. When I find him loading some of our timber into the back of his van before he leaves one evening, I am not convinced by his explanation that he is putting it there to keep it dry. We have words. He unloads it with bad grace, and chucks it in a puddle. We part on terms of mutual dislike.

With bookings already filling up most of the summer, I've started spending the deposit money to boost the building fund which is running low. I'm frantic.

An acquaintance introduces a big, broad-shouldered man with a disconcerting mannerism of looking over his own right shoulder when he talks, so that I speak to the side of his head. Wandering around the buildings, he pushes at the walls with his hands as if he expects them to fall down, scrapes with his foot at the floors, tutting and shaking his head.

"When were you wanting these places ready?"

"Our first bookings are for the second week of July."

He opens his eyes wide, then makes a puffing noise through pouted lips.

"Well, we'd better get on with it. What you need here is hands, and plenty of them."

I feel a glimmer of hope.

Next day he starts work, bringing with him his girlfriend, her brother and cousin, and two small dogs. One of them is adept at climbing ladders and scrambling about on beams, while the other, which is not, sits howling and whimpering in frustration.

No 4, as I mentally call him, is terrifyingly gung-ho. He prowls around with a screeching chainsaw searching for something to chop or lop. This morning he's up an oak sawing through the 12" trunk of ivy that is throttling the tree. He is balanced precariously on a branch, thrashing around with the machine like something from a horror film. Then he attacks some discarded beams, and chops them into slices for firewood. When he has run out of anything more to chop, he starts rectifying the mess created and left behind by monkey No. 3.

Addressing the two windows that have been perplexing me, he points out that they have no lintels, and are supporting the entire roof. They will have to come out, he says, and be replaced properly. But if he takes them out, won't the roof collapse, I ask. He taps the side of his nose, and tells me not to worry.

This chap is no monkey. He knows what he's doing, and he's getting on with it. He's quickly made himself at home, bounding into the kitchen every morning promptly at 8.00 am, whistling tunelessly and making himself and me a cup of Earl Grey and two slices of buttered toast, plus various refreshments for his team. They are hearty eaters and as they are all working for No. 4 and not being paid by me, I'm happy to keep them well fed.

With eleven weeks of bookings for the season, and work progressing as it is, we are well on schedule.

The peanut supply is diminishing rapidly, and we still have to furnish the cottages. I've bought new beds, cookers and fridges, and some easy chairs, but we need much more. I find a card in a local supermarket advertising "Quality furniture at sensible prices," and call the number.

A deep public school voice instructs: "If you wish to speak to Beverly, then please say so. If you wish to speak to Tristram, do so now."

I explain that I'm looking for decent inexpensive furniture for our holiday guests, and Tristram assures me that he has a warehouse of furniture that will be exactly what I am looking for. We arrange to meet twelve miles away at a place I have never heard of. He will wait for me at the crossroads, because, he assures me cheerfully, I'll never find his house by myself.

After driving through an endless network of narrow roads, past collections of houses where no sign of life stirs, numerous fields and scraggy copses, I am relieved to see an estate car parked at the agreed rendezvous with a man leaning against it. But not a man like any other. In bloodstock terms, he is 'by Viking out of Greek Goddess'.

He's tall and slender. His skin is the same golden copper as his cropped hair and trimmed beard. His blue eyes are fringed with thick black lashes. His nose is straight and narrow, and his broad smile shows startling white teeth. As I climb out of the car my leg bones threaten to melt. I offer a hot, sticky little paw to the outstretched golden hand with its slender fingers, and stand there foolishly and speechlessly.

"Do you like dogs?" he asks, opening the door of his car and releasing a torrent of smooth-haired dachshunds, sleek as otters.

"Meet the children. Children, say hello to our new friend."

The dogs prod my ankles with wet noses, tails wagging.

"Good. The children approve. Let's go."

He invites the children back into his car, and I follow him along a bumpy path through thick woods sinister in their dark stillness, quelling a momentary feeling of panic. What if he's a murderer or rapist? Nobody knows I'm here. They'll never find my body. Who will feed my animals? Even if I manage to escape, I'll never find my way back.

We break out of the woods into a field, and the path leads to a gravelled area in front of a house typical of the area, long and low, with two front doors and a pantiled roof. The walls are a light shade of apricot, the shutters a soft eau-de-nil.

Uncannily, as he opens my car door, Tristram says: "I expect you were getting worried about where you were going to end up!"

He ushers me into the living room. "Come."

After living on a building site for so long, I've almost forgotten what a normal home looks like. There are a few oriental rugs scattered on the flags, a couple of sofas flanking the fireplace, a pile of books on a low table. It's simple, comfortable, and tasteful.

"Be at home," says Tristram, waving a beautiful hand around vaguely.

"I expect you would love a glass of mint tea. Beverly! Come and meet our guest."

Through the patio doors comes a slightly older man - as blonde as Tristram, but shorter, stockier, clean-shaven, with smiling eyes.

"My partner," says Tristram. "Beverly, show Susie your garden. I shall join you shortly with something heavenly."

Beverly leads me through sliding glass doors onto a patio surrounded by flowerbeds, pergolas, climbing roses, a small pond, herbaceous borders and a bright green, velvety lawn. The smell of roses and honeysuckle fills the air. It's a perfect English country garden, in the middle of rural France - something that takes great skill and patience to achieve. Colours and shapes blend in harmony. We sit under a gazebo on a paved area.

"Are you a professional garden designer?" I ask. "It's heavenly."

"I was an accountant by profession, but a gardener at heart. It's taken me four years to create this. I've had to adapt many of my ideas – the climate here is too extreme for certain plants, but yes, I'm rather proud and pleased with the result."

It's an idyllic location, secluded and with unhindered views of fields and open countryside.

"It suits us, my dear. It's private."

Tristram arrives with frosted glasses of chilled mint tea, and we sit chatting while the children wrestle playfully around our feet.

"No, Pumpkin," he calls to one of the dogs who is tentatively trying to excavate a clump of campanula from between some edging stones.

"Shall we visit the emporium?" he asks when we've finished our tea.

"What is it you're after exactly?"

"Basic, practical stuff. Dining tables and chairs, side tables, book cases. It must be decent, but not expensive. Our budget's very tight."

"Right. Let's see what we've got." He leads the way to a large barn at right angles to the house, and hauls back a sliding door.

Daylight floods in onto stacks of packing crates and bulky shapes draped in blankets.

"That's the good stuff that keeps the wolf from the door. Over here is the rest."

There are acres of items of furniture, arranged in neat rows. It's a mixed bag: formica kitchen units with chrome dials, battered pine tables, chairs that need re-caning, baths, stoves, garden furniture, but also some relatively modern items.

"House clearances. Usually there will be at least a couple of good pieces that I sell on to dealers. And the rest, this kind of thing, well, you'd be surprised, but it goes, sooner or later. I've a contact who buys for film and TV sets. They're always looking out for stuff like this. And 60s items are coming into fashion again out here."

I pick out some basic items that, with a bit of love and effort, will do for the time being. Tristram will deliver them when I'm ready, for "a small consideration. " I don't like to ask how small.

As I drive away, he and Beverly wave from the doorway, standing beside each other, with the children at their feet. A scene of contentment and domestic bliss that gives me a warm fuzzy feeling.

The Gravel Mountain

By the end of April progress has slackened. Although the roofs, windows and doors are in place, the buildings are still empty shells. No. 4 insists there is no cause to worry. He has reduced his workforce to just himself and his girlfriend, who survives on a strict diet of coffee and Gitanes. She is as thin as a reed but impressively nimble and strong, carrying and lifting hods of tiles and buckets of cement without damaging her immaculate manicure or creasing her face. Sometimes it almost seems as if she is working harder than he is.

By the end of May the electrics and water services are all in place, but I am waking in a panic almost every night. A month doesn't seem long enough to tile the floors, put up the pine ceilings and paint the whole place, not to mention clearing up the mess outside and getting the garden planted. No. 4's girlfriend has disappeared, taking the small sad dog with her. Pouring his 20th cup of tea of the day, licking and dabbing his fingers into the biscuit box to mop up the last remaining crumbs, No. 4 promises we have time to spare. I should learn to relax and have faith. I want to, but I can't. He is constantly up and down and backwards and forwards. The chainsaw is always buzzing and the biscuit tin always empty and the tea always brewing, but I can't see any noticeable progress in the cottages.

Less than three weeks before the first guests arrive, No 4 leaves a phone message to say he and his girlfriend have taken the dogs on holiday "to the seaside," as the howling dog is suffering from depression. Both the cottages look like bombsites, with ladders, tools and sacks of plaster all over the place. I am now seriously stressed and can feel the blood pulsing in my ears and pumping around my body faster than it should. I trundle around with a wheelbarrow collecting rocks, broken tiles, lumps of superfluous concrete, bits of timber and lengths of cable and pipe, shovelling them into sacks to take to the tip. No 4's mobile phone is switched off, and his girlfriend's parents have no idea when they are likely to return. I consider taking up smoking.

Three days later, unrepentant and infuriatingly patronising, No. 4 returns with his ladder-climbing dog. He ignores my displeasure and actually pats me on the head, suggesting I bake a cake while he gets on with his work. In a fit of extreme pique I hide all biscuits and Earl Grey tea bags. Shortly afterwards he bounces chirpily into the kitchen, singing his monotonous five-note tune, and clicking the kettle on. Then there is much opening and closing of drawers, and finally he comes into the living room to say he can't find the tea bags. I tell him that until there is some visible progress on the building front, tea and biscuits are off the menu. He shrugs and bounces out again, humming. I don't see him for the rest of the day. I lay awake most of the night terrified he won't turn up in the morning.

Promptly at 8.00am he arrives, singing 'zippetty doo da,' waving a box of tea bags and a bag of *pains au chocolat*. Today, he announces, he will be tiling the floors while I make the tea. At the end of the day he can barely walk, but to his credit the entire ground floor of both buildings has been perfectly tiled. And he has had a brainwave, an inspiration, for a time-saving, labour-saving way of grouting them. Instead of the conventional laborious mixing of grout and spreading into the joints with a scraper, he will pour a very wet cement mix over the entire floor, allowing it to flow into the cracks. Once it has set and dried, he will wipe over the tiles with a cloth to remove the excess. He estimates this could save two days work. I'm apprehensive at the thought of the floors smothered in wet cement, but we desperately need to save time.

Next morning he is sloshing buckets of runny cement all over the newly tiled floors. The liquid doesn't flow, but lays in a sullen grey puddle. We have to wade about in it and push it around with lengths of wood, and it makes a simply dreadful mess. By next day it has formed a thick gritty coating covering the entire ground floor of both buildings. After rubbing vigorously with a dry cloth, No 4 admits gloomily that it hasn't worked out quite as he hoped. He won't have time to rectify it as well as fitting the kitchens and ceiling panelling and painting all the walls. He passes the floor problem to me.

It takes three days, with buckets of soapy water, cloths, scrubbing brushes and abrasive pads. While the tiles are wet it looks as if all traces of cement have gone, but as soon as they dry a new grey veil emerges. I have to continually wet the cement and rub it very hard to make any impression, whilst avoiding rubbing the cracks because the grouting is still soft and smears itself over the tiles into a new mess. And hour after hour the humming continues as No 4 makes endless tea, as I am permanently bent double and there are still acres of floor to clean. Scrubbing and rubbing, I start hating No 4 with a fearsome passion.

By the end of the week the kitchen units are installed, the ceilings are in place, and the floors are as clean and free of cement as they are ever going to be. No 4 has done well, and when he comes for his weekly wages he asks whether he may have an advance against his next and final week, as he has a problem with his car and is short of cash. I make an exception to my primal rule of never paying a builder before the work is completed. In spite of everything, he has accomplished almost all that I have asked, so I pay him for the following week.

Next week he will be back to paint all the walls, and fill the courtyards with the twelve cubic yards of crushed limestone he has ordered for the purpose.

When he hasn't shown by mid-day on Monday, and his mobile phone is switched off, I know I've been taken for a ride and have only myself to blame. I begin painting, and I paint from early morning to the small hours of the following morning, until I can barely see, but I get the first coat on the ceilings and walls in both cottages. After a few hours sleep I pick flakes of paint out of my hair and off my face and hands, and start all over again.

The gravel didn't arrive this morning as promised. I call the quarry, who say the delivery is on its way.

Late in the afternoon a truck arrives and begins spewing a mountain of large sharp grey granite pieces. Shouting, waving my arms and making violent throat-slashing signs, I manage to stop the cascade. Half of it is already spreading over the drive. The surly driver insists I ordered granite, not limestone. I call the quarry and they ask me to pass him the phone. After some furious conversation he shovels the stuff back onto his truck and drives away spitting curses and muttering "*quelle pute anglaise.*" The quarry phone back to say they will be here at 9.00am tomorrow with the limestone.

The following morning they phone again, saying the truck has broken down, and then in the afternoon they are short of a driver, but they'll be here tomorrow morning without fail.

I'm woken next day by a crashing and whooshing noise. It sounds as if the buildings are collapsing. Leaping to the window I see a vast truck expelling a torrent of crushed limestone just inside the gate. And as I watch another truck drives up and spews out a second heap, forming a mountain range which cuts off my car, house and the cottages from the rest of the world. There is enough gravel to give the entire hamlet a generous coating.

It's already hot. The air is still. The only sounds are the droning of the bees and chirping of the crickets. I find No. 4's shovel, and a battered wheelbarrow, and start shovelling and tipping. The gravel is only about twenty yards from where it needs to go, but it might as well be twenty miles. The shovel is heavy and the limestone is heavy and the wheelbarrow is heavy. After two hours, it is impossibly hot. The tarmac is melting. The garden is wilting. I can barely lift the shovel. Every few minutes I step back from the pile to see if there is any noticeable difference. There isn't. I recognise the impossibility of moving it all by tomorrow. Staring at it bleakly, I curse No 4 with an intensity that frightens me. Then I burst into tears of rage and frustration.

What am I going to do? I bawl. The dogs sniff and lick me as I sit on the pile, jabbing my heels angrily into the stones.

A car engine stops on the other side of the gravel mountain. There's a lot of crunching, and over the top appears Tristram who slithers down onto the driveway. I'd forgotten he's delivering the furniture today.

"My dear girl, what on earth has happened? What have you done? You look dreadful!"

I throw myself at him, sobbing, and waving hopelessly at the heap of limestone.

"Why don't we have a lovely glass of mint tea?" he asks, tactfully disentangling my damp dirty hands from his crisp white shirt. "You'll find it really does make everything better."

By the time I have picked some mint, torn it up, put it in the pot, sprinkled it with sugar and left it to steep, Tristram has taken off his shirt and is shovelling heroically, singing snatches from Rigoletto in his deep baritone. I want to fling my arms around him again and kiss him all over, but I'm not sure he'd appreciate it.

"I've given Bev a call. He'll be here soon."

Beverly arrives with the children, who make instant friends with our very sociable dogs and go and lie in the cool of the house with them. We dig out a second wheelbarrow and another shovel, and between the two of them, fuelled with gallons of mint tea and cucumber and tomato sandwiches, by late afternoon the mountain has been moved and the courtyards are carpeted with nearly knee-deep limestone chippings. There is no time to hire a compactor, and anyway it wouldn't be any use. As Tristram points out after we have bashed at the stuff with the back of the shovels and jumped up and down on it to no effect, there is far too much of it.

"Why did you order so much? And it's the wrong grade, far too coarse. It will never compact into a smooth surface."

"It's going to be hell to walk on," Beverly adds helpfully.

As a matter of fact, it's virtually impossible. Like trudging over very deep, very thick sand. As you drag your feet out your shoes fill with little pebbles. We stare gloomily at it, willing it to vanish. Tristram remarks playfully that it will certainly anchor the garden furniture in place.

They are both streaked with dust and sweat.

"You won't mind if we rinse ourselves off?" Tristram points to our garden hosepipe.

"Perhaps you'd like me to do your backs?" I suggest.

"Get thee behind us, Satan!" he laughs. "And make more mint tea."

Once they're refreshed, we unload the furniture and put it in place. It looks better than I had expected.

"Nice. Most pleasant. Your guests will love it here," says Beverly. "It's a lovely location. I can give you some plants, too, so that you can pretty the garden. I've plenty of cuttings and seedlings."

Later we sit by candlelight listening to the nightingales, eating a Greek salad and sipping, as a change from mint tea, a bottle of Sancerre that Beverly thoughtfully brought with him. I reflect on how very lucky and privileged I am to count as friends these two kind and charming men.

"Do the cottages have names?" asks Beverly.

"Yes. The larger one is Lavande, and the little one Pissenlit. I've got a couple of ceramic name plaques on order."

They both look rather startled. "Pissenlit? Do you know what that means?"

"Yes. It's French for dandelion," I say, straight-faced.

"But surely you know how it actually translates," insists Beverly.

"No," I lie. "Tell me."

Beverly coughs. "Well, literally, it means 'piss in the bed'."

"Well I never. I hope nobody does," I reply.

Tristram catches my eye. "Naughty! You knew perfectly well. I think you have a somewhat contorted sense of humour."

Neither he nor Beverly will accept anything for their help today.

"An absolute pleasure. And any time you are in need, you have only to ask."

It's 11.00pm by the time they leave. The last thing I have to do is varnish the staircases in both cottages. It only takes an hour. The brush starts falling to pieces, and a few bristles remain embedded for eternity in the varnish, like insects in amber. But I don't think anybody will notice. We're open for business!

The First Guests

Apart from one of the cats having diarrhoea behind the washing machine, everything is under control and organised. I've put a dozen pots of vivid geraniums in each courtyard, set up the garden furniture and barbecues, and filled vases with sunflowers, welcome baskets with tea, coffee and fruit, and the fridge with croissants, butter, jam, milk and a bottle of wine. There are stacks of brochures on local attractions, lists of recommended restaurants, a pile of books and board games. By early afternoon, we are ready for our first guests, six young men who have booked Lavande for a fortnight. Does this portend drunken orgies, blaring rap music and a smashed-up house? Is it going to be a baptism of fire for a novice landlady?

Confusingly they all look virtually identical when they arrive, like a litter of puppies. All with neat hair cuts, all wearing odd, low-slung, baggy shorts, trainers and T-shirts with slogans on them: *Out of my mind - back shortly. Rich bitch wanted - apply here. Save water - drink beer.*

They politely shake hands and introduce themselves. Three of them are called Chris: Tall Chris, Skinny Chris and Chris, who is also tall. They all thank me for having them, and unload half a dozen cardboard cartons from the back of their people carrier.

An hour later barbecue scents waft into the air, and I can hear bottles chinking. Apart from conversation and laughter, and sometimes the clink of glass or popping of a cork, that's all the noise I hear from the cottage during their stay. Occasionally they pile into their car and disappear for a couple of hours, and they spend a whole day at Monkey Valley, but mostly they just hang around in the garden, playing with the cats, chatting and laughing. Twice they offer to take the dogs for a walk, and once they ask if I need anything from town. Every day they neatly peg out their washing on the line. I'd love to know what they do in real life, but if guests don't volunteer information, I don't ask.

When they leave at the end of the fortnight, they knock on the door to say farewell, thank me for having them, tell me they all love the cats, and present me with an enormous fruit tart and a little card that says: "Thank you, missus. We've had a great time. See you next year."

In the guest book each of them has written, in different coloured ink, some vertically, and one diagonally across the page: "I love monkeys. And cats." They've left Lavande looking like a show home. They've even cleaned the windows, and left behind in the fridge an unopened bottle of wine, some butter, a packet of bacon, a few bits of fruit and some salad. In the living room I find neat piles of paperback books and magazines with a note saying they hope future guests will enjoy them.

I notice that the varnish on the staircase is peeling off in a few places and looks rather scabby. So I have a good idea – I will rub it down with sandpaper and quickly put a new coat on. The tin says it dries in an hour. But it doesn't. It's still tacky at 4.00pm. Maybe I didn't stir the tin thoroughly enough? By six it's touch dry, but when I prod it with a matchstick, it leaves a small dip. Perhaps it wasn't meant for staircases.

It's almost 8.00pm when an elderly Mercedes pulls up and out climbs a big, shambling man with lank grey hair, and a dainty woman with a blonde elfin hairstyle, peaches and cream complexion and chic, with expensive rings on every finger, a necklace, several bracelets, a brooch and dangling earrings, and a voice that could shatter glass at half a mile.

The chic lady introduces them: Alice and Dick. "Let's get to know you," she suggests. "We'll have a drink with you while we recover from the journey."

Scrunching over the courtyard towards the patio, Alice says forthrightly, "Oh, I don't like this gravel. It's going to ruin my shoes." She bends her shapely leg to examine the heels of her stilettos, and her short tight skirt rises to reveal some black and red lacy suspenders. She is either unaware, or unabashed.

"Would you like tea?" I ask.

"I'll have a beer," replies Dick. "In fact," he laughs, "I'll have a couple."

"You'll go and get my Burberry bag out of the car first," Alice tells him. He heaves himself up onto his slightly bowed legs entwined with thick, triffid-like veins. Long yellow toenails poking out from his sandals remind me of Rosa Kreb's shoes with the daggers in the toes in 'From Russia with Love'.

Alice must have caught my expression, because as he ambles towards the gate she says, "Not beautiful, is he? But very useful when I need a chauffeur and porter. And *very* obedient. Never underestimate the value of an ugly man. " She wiggles her little finger, and winks.

"What would you like to drink?" I ask, and intending to continue "tea, coffee, soft drink or beer?" But Alice beats me to it.

"I'll have a Nuits-St-Georges if you have some. In a big glass, please. I always have a big glass."

I gulp and apologise that we do not have any Nuits-St-Georges. The best I can offer her is an excellent Sauvignon from the Domaine de Villemont, an Haut Poitou vineyard about 30 miles away. It is in the fridge waiting for a special occasion. But I somehow can't bring myself to offer Alice the cheap plonk we keep for every day.

Sprawling in his chair, Dick knocks back his first beer with one slurp and tosses the empty bottle into a flowerbed with a belch. I try not to look at his feet.

Alice sniffs her wine, swirls it around the glass, sips, sucks, and says, "Hm. I wouldn't buy it, personally, but it'll do. Dick will have to get me some St Georges tomorrow." She gulps it down and holds out her glass for a refill. With every move she makes, her jewellery jangles a merry little tune like a tastefully decorated musical Christmas tree. The only time she isn't talking is when she's drinking.

I mention the staircase, and ask if they would mind very much not walking on it in their shoes until tomorrow, when it should be completely dry.

"It will be fine with bare feet, but I think the surface is still just a little soft and might not stand up to shoes."

"My darling daughter," Alice says, "has a very expensive house. She earns a huge salary; so does her husband. Both their children are gifted and go to private schools, don't they Dick? She's had the whole house re-decorated by the most exclusive company in the south of England. Hand-made oak kitchen units; real marble floors in the bathrooms - there are four bathrooms, aren't there, Dick?"

She twitters on for several minutes. Dick holds out his empty bottle to me, saying "Top up, love."

While I'm in the kitchen Alice's chattering continues unabated, all about her daughter's splendid house, the landscaped gardens and covered swimming pool.

"Of course, she has a contractor to deal with it. She doesn't have time, and neither does Alan. They have *very* important jobs. A man comes in to do the cleaning and service the pumps and filters. And of course, he has to make sure that the PHD of the water is just right, doesn't he Dick? I think it's the PHD. Anyway, it's something like that."

Dick grunts and mutters under his breath: "pH, you silly tart."

Alice ignores him.

"Did she have her staircase varnished?" I ask, trying to form a link between our staircase and her daughter.

"Of course not. The cleaner waxes it. It's Jacobean oak."

When there are no beers left in the fridge, and the Sauvignon bottle is empty, I take them over to Lavande.

"Pretty. Nice colour scheme. My darling daughter..."

I nip her daughter quickly in the bud and show them around. We all take off our shoes to go upstairs, and none of us stick to the steps.

Dick has become rather red-faced and loud, and pulls Alice towards him, then bends her over the back of the settee and tries to heave her skirt up.

"Behave yourself, you old goat," she snaps, but she gives me a wink.

"Can't get enough. I've always had that effect on men. Dick knows, don't you Dick?"

"Well, I'll leave you to settle in. Please give me a shout if you need anything – and if you could please remember about taking off your shoes on the staircase."

Alice assures me that they'll take off their shoes, then she flicks a finger at Dick and says, "Go and get the rest of my things in from the car, and make us something to eat. I'm going to do my nails."

I eat a packet of biscuits, take a quick shower then climb into to bed, falling asleep the moment I close my eyes. Later a frightful noise rends the night and wakes me with a start. Tannhauser, at full volume. My watch says 3.25 am. The noise goes on for hours. The dogs howl in harmony. It sounds as if Dick and Alice are settling in nicely.

Next morning, sitting bleary-eyed in the garden sipping coffee and inhaling the early sunshine, with the dogs and cats at my feet, I hear Dick and Alice's car disappearing down the road, and drowse for an hour, enjoying an opportunity to relax.

Our first Pissenlit guests missed their flight from Belfast to London, and consequently don't arrive until mid-afternoon on Sunday. James and Ellen are a young recently-married couple from Belfast, who don't want to be in their home town during the Orange Day parade.

"Things happen, you know. It can get violent. We don't like that sort of thing."

James' broad accent takes a while to get to grips with, but once I tune in I find it seductive. Ellen speaks very softly, in a similar accent, and never takes her eyes from his cheerful face.

"Will you look at that!" He points to a large bumblebee creature exploring a crevice in the wall.

"It's got a red arse! Did you ever hear of a red-arsed bumblebee before?"

He breaks off a lavender stalk and tries to encourage the creature onto it, but after a few moments it buzzes away. James shakes his head in wonderment. "Well, I never. A bloody red-arsed bee."

After they've unpacked, they wander into the garden and ask if they may have a look round. They are both townies, and while Ellen is very timid, James is fearless, loves the dogs and is fascinated by wildlife. Neither have ever had a pet, and James has asked if they can "adopt" the dogs while they're here. The dogs need no enticement. They'll worship anybody who says "Hello," particularly if there's anything edible within range. James holds Ellen by the hand and reassures her while the dogs snuffle around her. She has absolute faith in James. I think if he told her to jump from the roof so that he could catch her, she wouldn't hesitate.

Next he's off to meet the horses, trotting right up behind one of them and patting her on the backside, startling her. Thankfully our two old mares are as gentle as kittens, but I suggest that they might be better approached from the front end.

"Would they be needing a brushing?" asks James. With their glossy summer coats they look spotless and polished, but I give him a body brush and leave him happily brushing and chattering away, with Ellen watching apprehensively from behind the gate.

Alice and Dick return with a car-load of shopping bags. Alice is already chattering before she gets out of the car. From twenty yards I can see her mouth moving non-stop. "...said to him that if he wants me to go to the Gambia with him, I'll need the right clothes. We found a beautiful boutique - very expensive - and he bought me four chiffon blouses. So chic, and terribly useful. You can wear them with anything. And two pairs of flat shoes - one black, one gold. So adaptable. Oh, by the way, I forgot about the stairs and walked on them yesterday evening with my shoes. But I don't think I've done any damage. Dick, go and pour me a big glass of Muscadet."

I love her style.

The Ride of the Valkyries jerks me awake just after 2.00 am. 15 minutes later a broad Irish voice calls out politely across the courtyard. "I wonder could you turn that fecking noise down, please. No offence, friends, but we're trying to sleep."

Alice's fingernail-on-blackboard voice screeches back: "So sorry. We're sozzled. Go to sleep, my love. Dick, turn it off."

Dick mumbles loudly and crashes into something, cursing, and after a few seconds silence reigns. Bliss.

Extract from '*Swallows And Robins – The Guests In My Garden*' by Susie Kelly

For links to Amazon Kindle USA, Amazon Kindle UK & Paperback sales pages please go to
http://blackbird-digitalbooks.com

 and click on the book cover.

COPYRIGHT

ABOUT THE AUTHOR

Born a Londoner, Susie Kelly spent most of the first 25 years of her life in Kenya. She now lives in south-west France with her husband and assorted animals. She's slightly scatterbrained and believes that compassion, courage and a sense of humour are the three essentials for surviving life in the 21st century. She gets on best with animals, eccentrics, and elderly people.

CONNECT WITH SUSIE KELLY
http://about.me/susie.kelly

Keep up to date with Susie Kelly news and new books by joining the Susie Kelly mailing list.
Email your contact details to
blackbird-digibooks@gmail.com
(Managed securely by Mailchimp, details are never, ever shared with any third parties)

SUSIE KELLY BOOKS

Best Foot Forward – A 500-Mile Walk Through Hidden France (Transworld 2000/Blackbird 2011) A touching and inspiring tale of the Texan pioneering spirit, English eccentricity, and two women old enough to know better.

The Valley of Heaven and Hell – Cycling in the Shadow of Marie-Antoinette (Blackbird 2011) Novice cyclist Susie bikes 500 miles through Paris and Versailles, the battlefields of World War 1, the Champagne region and more

Two Steps Backward (Bantam 2004) The trials and tribulations of moving a family and many animals from the UK to a run-down smallholding in SW France.

Travels With Tinkerbelle, 6,000 Miles Around France In A Mechanical Wreck (Blackbird 2012) The author and her husband devised a simple plan – to take a tent and the dog and drive around the perimeter of France. Like many simple plans it went wrong before it started.

Swallow & Robins (Blackbird 2012) The true story of a beginner's attempts at running two holiday homes in remotest France and her love/hate relationship with her guests. (Blackbird 2013)

I Wish I Could Say I Was Sorry... (Blackbird 2013) Susie's heartbreaking childhood memoir set in 1950s London and Kenya. An Amazon.com Top 100 title.

Available from Amazon as Kindle Ebooks & Paperbacks

MORE
BLACKBIRD DIGITAL BOOKS

The Dream Theatre by Sarah Ball (2011)
A London Steal – The Fabulous-On-A-Budget Guide to London's Hidden Chic by Elle Ford (2013)
The Cat Name Book by Christina Hamilton (2012)
The Widow's To Do List by Stephanie Zia (2011)
How To Be A Literary Genius (2013) by Jacqui Lofthouse
On Foot Across France: Dunkerque to The Pyrenees (2014) by Tim Salmon

Blackbird Digital Books
London
http://blackbird-digitalbooks.com/
blackbird.digibooks@gmail.com

Printed in Great Britain
by Amazon